About people

GW00630932

About people

About people
What the Bible says

Derek Williams

Inter-Varsity Press

INTER-VARSITY PRESS
Universities and Colleges Christian Fellowship
38 De Montfort Street, Leicester LE1 7GP, England
© Derek L. Williams, 1977
First edition 1977
ISBN 0 85110 399 5
Quotations from the Bible are from the Revised
Standard Version (copyrighted 1946 and 1952,
second edition 1971, by the Division of Christian
Education, National Council of the Churches of
Christ in the United States of America).
Set in 11pt Bembo
Printed in Great Britain by
Hunt Barnard Printing Ltd.,
Aylesbury, Bucks.

Contents

'*Have I not reason to lament*
What man has made of man?'
(Wordsworth)

'*Philosophy is not the concern of those who pass through Divinity and Greats, but of those who pass through birth and death. If the ordinary man may not discuss existence, why should he be asked to conduct it?*'
(G. K. Chesterton)

'*We care what happens to people only in proportion as we know what people are.*'
(Henry James)

Prologue

A sandwich bar which I frequent in the city centre has a card propped up over the soup tins. Beside a drawing of a haggard businessman is the assertion, 'I am a human being,' and the injunction, 'Do not fold, spindle or mutilate.' Official forms sometimes carry the same injunction.

The message is obvious. As human beings, we instinctively feel that we are of more value than a piece of paper to be processed at will by someone else. That does not, however, make it any easier for us to see anything more in our television window on the world than a feelingless sea of faces in a celluloid crowd. Even the people who bring our milk and mail, those who clip our tickets or check our purchases at the till, we regard more as convenient servants and not as complex humans. We live in an impersonal society; it is hard for us not to be impersonal in our thinking.

This is especially true when we read a book. A hundred mass-distributed pages of mechanically-printed words which could, for all you know, have been written by a computer or a chimpanzee. So let me assure you right at the beginning that I, like you, am a human being. I am just under six feet tall, rather skinny, short-sighted and thirty-one years old. I feel pain when someone pinches me, tiredness after a day's work, and happiness when I put my feet up to watch football on the telly.

Unfortunately, I know nothing about you. Not even your name. A book is a one-way means of communication. By the time you have finished, you will have learned quite a few things about me. I, however, will have learned nothing about your hobbies and hopes, your hang-ups and habits, about all those things which go to make you a unique person. All I do know is that, because you are a human being, you know what it is to live a human life, loving and learning, caring and crying, being angry, and just plain *being*.

This shared experience of being human is my concern in writing to you. Rarely do we stop to ask what is the essence of our humanity, and when we do we rarely know an answer. As I sit here, making marks on a piece of paper, can I believe that I am anything more than a chance collection of atoms behaving in a highly developed yet purely mechanical manner? As you sit reading, perhaps surrounded by your family, perhaps alone in a draughty bed-sit, is it very likely that you have any significance in a world which seems like an infinitesimal speck of cosmic dust floating in the incomprehensible depths of eternity? As we play and laugh together in the sun, mourn beside a grave, grieve over our mistakes, gasp at the sight of snow-capped mountains, bathe in the warmth of human love, dare we say that our feelings are more than mere animal instincts and chemical reactions? Just what is it that makes us the people we are, or prevents us from being the people we long to be?

These are not idle questions. They are not the sole province of disinterested intellectuals philosophizing in their academic ivory towers. They profoundly affect you and me. Suppose you are someone whose work is with people: a nurse or a personnel officer, or a teacher. Your answers to the basic questions of what a person really is will directly affect the way you approach the next one you have to deal with. Perhaps you are a planner or an architect, an engineer or a builder; then your conception of human needs and requirements will affect the very shape and structure of the things you produce for people – things which will profoundly influence them for good or ill. If you are a sportsman or a student, or just an ordinary nobody, your understanding of human nature will affect all the words, actions and attitudes which make your little world go round.

So important is the subject that Emil Brunner, a Swiss theologian, asserts that

> the fact that binds together the most influential thinkers of recent generations, those whose thought was capable of determining the thought, not only of other thinkers, but of the masses, and through them determining the whole course of political development, Charles Darwin, Friedrich Nietzsche, and Karl Marx, was this: that each of them gained power directly or indirectly over a considerable section of mankind, by his view of man, by his anthropology.[1]

Now let me make one thing clear. I am not writing any brand new theories about the human condition. 'The answer everyone has waited for! You, too, can be a Twenty-First Century Man now!' If that is what you want, you will find plenty of charlatans who will provide it. I am not one of them; I happen to believe that real life is a little more complicated than such a simplistic approach would suggest.

I am writing to tell you what the Bible has to say about human nature. Within its pages we discover a wholly consistent picture of human nature which is neither excessively romantic nor unduly pessimistic. It offers to men and women of every culture, class and century a coherent understanding of humanity and a workable way of life which has stood the tests of market place and palace, and which embraces every detail of daily existence. The insights of philosophers and the observations of psychologists and physiologists have contributed much to our understanding of mankind, but none have dared to suggest anything quite so potentially meaningful and dynamic as the biblical conception of the whole man.

If I had the space to do so, I would want to argue that the reason for this is that the Bible is a unique statement by God about himself and the world. As it is, I am content to leave this question on one side, and just explain, as simply as I know how, what the Bible actually says about the nature of man. Even if you have doubts about the inspiration of Scripture, you can hardly deny that it has been influential, and it is worth considering for that reason alone. Indeed, I am not even assuming just because you are reading an unashamedly Christian book, that you are yourself a Christian – although I hope that by the time you have finished it you will see both yourself and the Christian faith in a clearer light.

C. S. Lewis once said that he wrote his novels because they were the kind of stories which he himself would enjoy reading. As a hardened commuter, habitually struggling through books which match the train for stuffiness, I have attempted to write something which even I could cope with amidst the bouncing clatter of a journey. It is not, therefore, a theological treatise. Indeed, the subject is so vast that I can only hope to introduce you to it and leave to others the more detailed exposition. For the reader who wishes to pursue the subject further, I have added questions and Bible references at the end of each chapter, and a suggested reading list at the end of the book. The chapter headings are for our convenience only; the Bible never categorizes man as neatly as I have done, but treats him as a complex whole. As we look at the various sections of the picture, we must never confuse them for the whole. And, to avoid misunderstanding, I should point out that my use of 'man' is merely a literary variation for 'person' or 'the human race'!

Now we are ready to begin. What follows is not a theoretical concept of humanity, something applicable to 'them', that universal scapegoat for all ills and inconveniences. It is not a precise formula, beloved of our technological mentality, which denies the very humanity it seeks to define. This book is about the person tapping the typewriter keys, and the person holding the completed book; it is about you and me.

Reference

[1] Emil Brunner, *Man in revolt* (Lutterworth Press, 1939), p.34.

'*Some of the sceptical methods applied to the world's origin might be applied to my origin, and a grave and earnest enquirer come to the conclusion that I was never born at all.*'
(G. K. Chesterton)

'*Thou madest man, he knows not why.*'
(Tennyson)

I

Man made

A tin of corned beef, 'Produce of the Argentine'. A watch, 'Precision made by Swiss craftsmen'. A nylon shirt, 'Made in England'. A plastic toy boat, 'Made in Hong Kong'.

Knowing about the origin of an article provides a guide to assessing its value. You will probably be willing to spend more money on a Swiss watch than a Hong Kong toy boat, because you expect the watch to be accurate and long-lasting, and assume that the boat has been mass-produced for the stocking-filler market. If, however, the *boat* were 'precision made by Swiss craftsmen', you might look again at what is possibly a working scale model designed to give you hours of pleasure.

We sometimes assess people in a similar way. An employer looking for a brainy recruit will prefer the applicant with a first-class honours degree to the school leaver with average exam results. The new bursar who starts work next week, having been an army officer for twenty years, is likely to be precise and punctual, polite but impatient.

When we come to discuss people as human beings we find that this rule-of-thumb assessment based on origins becomes difficult. Certainly, man interprets his place in the cosmos in accordance with the conclusions he reaches concerning his history and development. But which conclusions are right? The theories of man's origins differ so widely that the little child's question, 'Mummy, where do people come from?' is never given a satisfactory, conclusive answer. The result is not merely a bewildered child; it is a bewildered race.

If you and I are inhabitants of a globe which itself began as a tiny ball bouncing around the roulette wheel of physical forces, and which has now come to rest on the lucky number of human life, then we are mere accidents. Unwanted, un-needed children born of chaos and chance, totally at the mercy of the blind fury of fate, we create cultures and creeds to enclose the brief moment of our appearance on earth and to shield our minds from the stark truth. Or, if we are merely sophisticated products grown from some primeval soup, then it is questionable if we can ever be truly termed 'persons'. We are just intelligent, feeling, *things*, different in degree, but not in kind, from trees and toads. Like so many busy bees, instinct drives us to build our human hives – and then we praise ourselves for our superiority.

If, however, we are the deliberate creation of a personal God, then there must be some real purpose to our existence (even if we have not yet discovered it). The uniqueness we feel as a species will not be the product of a corporate imagination seeking to explain itself, but a real, designed uniqueness. The personalities we each possess will not be characterless combinations of chemicals but the real designs of a divine artist.

> A universe that has no divine Creator – the universe assumed in the theory of mechanistic evolution – never could make sense because it never would have been designed to have any.[1]

That is how one Bible commentator sums up the problem. The British Humanist Association concludes: 'We do not believe there is any ultimate purpose to life, nor think there is any point in looking for one.'[2] But the ordinary person cannot escape the conviction that the philosophy of 'Eat, drink and be merry, for tomorrow we die' is unutterably shallow. Even humanists who deny ultimate purposes live as if there were at least *temporary* ones; self-sacrifice is much more part of their official creed than self-indulgence. But temporary purposes have no meaning unless they relate to more permanent ones; which is where the Bible begins its account of human nature. God, it tells us, made man, and that makes all the difference.

God, genes and Genesis

Throughout the Bible, only one thing is assumed without detailed explanation, and that is the existence of God. The God we discover revealed within its pages is not remote and incomprehensible; he is involved in human affairs, discloses his character and purposes to men, and invites the individual into a direct relationship with him. Everything and everyone is discussed in the light of the one to whom they owe their own existence. 'In the beginning God created the heavens and the earth' (Genesis 1:1); 'All things were made through him' (John 1:3); 'By thy will they existed and were created' (Revelation 4:11).

The long-standing debate between Christianity and science has not primarily concerned the detailed interpretation of certain passages of the book of Genesis, but the existence and operations of a creator God. It is generally agreed that as Genesis pulls back the curtains to give us a glimpse of the dawn of life, what we see is not so much a documentary film report as an artist's impression. The shapes and outlines are accurate, but they are not detailed; they convey principles, not precise analyses, of truth. That does not, however, prevent this outburst by a popular scientific writer:

It is difficult to imagine a god of any kind occupying himself creating, by some spiritual micro-chemistry, a molecule of deoxyribonucleic acid which enabled the primitive ancestral

17

organism to grow and multiply. The whole hypothesis has come to its natural end in absurdity.[3]

Of course, it *is* difficult to imagine God or to comprehend his creative acts; God is so much greater than our minds. But we can neither demonstrate nor disprove his existence by examining some minute part of his universe in the laboratory. An amateur mechanic would not dream of disputing the existence of Fords just because he had successfully stripped down his Cortina and put it together again with the help of some home-made parts! The existence of God is something we should discuss, but if we are to remain logical and rational we must turn to Jesus' claims that he himself revealed God.

The Bible writers have a dynamic view of God; that is, they see him at work not only in the origin of life on the earth, but in the birth and growth of every individual (and they were not ignorant of the normal means of procreation). 'For thou didst form my inward parts, thou didst knit me together in my mother's womb' (Psalm 139:13). 'It is he who made us' (Psalm 100:3). The eighteenth-century Deists believed that God created the world like a watch; he wound it up and then let it run by itself. Not so the Bible writers; God has created a 'fixed order' (Jeremiah 31:35) operating according to certain laws, but he is not an absent landlord. 'My father is working still, and I am working' claimed Jesus (John 5:17). The prophet asserts that the Lord 'who spread forth the earth and what comes from it, . . . *gives* breath to the people upon it' (Isaiah 42:5), whilst Paul quotes a non-Christian poet to point up the truth that 'in him we live and move and have our being' (Acts 17:28).

Despite the highly organized industrial complexes, and the high-yielding agricultural systems; despite the sweat and toil exerted by every family breadwinner, you and I none the less owe our moment-by-moment existence to the God who is 'upholding the universe by his word of power' (Hebrews 1:3). Despite the population pouring its teeming millions over the face of the earth, despite the fact that many in that human sea were never wanted by their parents and are of no concern to their rulers save for the taxes they pay and the guns they wield, each individual can say 'I am a human being made by God. I therefore have a real value; I matter in the world.'*

Not everyone wants to say that, of course, but the fact that they nevertheless stand in a relationship to God as his creatures is not changed. Even when his purposes are incomprehensible, when his love seems questionable, the living creator-God stands over against man and this knowledge provides the beginning of an answer to the questions we ask about ourselves in God's world.

> Always, wherever, whatever, however,
> When I am able to resist
> For once the constant pressure of the failure to exist,
> Let me remember
> That truly to be man is man aware of Thee
> And unafraid to be. So help me God.[4]

Adam and Eve and the Andamanese

Everyone has heard of Adam and Eve. Their story is read every Christmas, although precisely what it has to do with cakes, cribs and candles is not always made clear. In the face of modern research, some Christians have become acutely embarrassed by the assertions of Genesis about man's origins, yet are unable to escape the place given by Jesus and Paul to the historical

---

* This would not be altered even if certain current biological experiments were successful, and man himself 'created' human life artificially. Methods such as 'cloning' (building an identical twin from a cell taken from the donor) and the fertilization and growth of embryos outside the womb, utilize human matter which is already alive (having God-given life, see chapter 7) and the result would be human as defined in chapter 3, although cloned twins would admittedly face an unprecedented identity crisis.

reality of Adam. Jesus quotes from the story, 'From the beginning (God) made them male and female' (Matthew 19:4). Paul makes the actions of Adam the basis for his teaching on man's relationship to God, and compares the historicity of Adam with that of Christ: 'as in Adam all die, so also in Christ shall all be made alive' (1 Corinthians 15:22). In his sermon to the intelligentsia of Athens, he claims that God 'made from one every nation of men' (Acts 17:26).

The account of Adam and Eve is undeniably ancient, and the folklore of many cultures has similar stories. The Andamanese Islanders, for instance, have one about the first man who was placed in a jungle paradise and forbidden to eat certain fruits. Some of his descendants disobeyed the command, were punished, and eventually destroyed by a flood. The original inhabitants of China, the Miao, said that death entered the world through a woman who ate forbidden white strawberries.

This has led some scholars to assert that Genesis is simply a legend among legends, invented by primitive man to explain certain deep problems of human existence. The similarity between the accounts is due, we are told, to 'archetypal images', patterns of symbolic thought which are common to men the world over. There is, however, an equally plausible explanation: that something really happened upon which all the narratives are based.

The memories of cataclysmic events linger for many generations. They are passed from father to son and become part of general knowledge. But the accounts are not only historical records; they are concepts imprinted on the psyche of the people. For example, an event as momentous as the Roman invasion of Britain leaves its mark on all future generations. Not only do our twentieth-century language, legal system, and road and settlement network reflect parts of the culture Caesar brought with him; as a people we would be totally different if he had not come. It is not inconceivable that the special circumstances surrounding the first humans, and the impact their actions had on future generations, gave birth to the traditions.

The early chapters of Genesis are deliberately given historical flavour. The location of Eden is somewhere in Mesopotamia, between the river Tigris and Euphrates (Genesis 2:10f.). Adam is a cultivator, and agriculture, including animal husbandry, is part of life outside Eden also (2:15; 4:2). Cain builds a settled community (4:17) and his descendants Jubal (a musician) and Tubal-cain (a metallurgist) developed the culture still further. The setting is very similar to that to which scholars have traced the birthplace of modern man. Some 10,000 years ago in Mesopotamia, *homo sapiens* appeared for the very first time. The last ice age was over and the nomadic men of that time settled into village life. Collecting and hunting gave way to cultivating and herding. A hybrid wheat which depends entirely upon man for its propagation was developed and metal goods were soon becoming common.

We have no need, therefore, to dismiss Adam and Eve as the imaginative creations of an ancient Hans Christian Andersen. The Genesis account is still more like a painting than a film, but it depicts some of the most important truths of the Bible. The teaching cannot be separated from the history. As in the rest of Scripture, God reveals his truth through the ordinary lives and circumstances of real people.

In the early chapters of Genesis we are introduced to the first man and woman who were made aware of God's character and nature. We watch their first moral questionings and decisions (which we shall concentrate on in the next chapter). And in Adam and Eve we discover that not only does the human race owe its existence to God; we also discover that it had a definite beginning in history. This is very important to many of the Bible writers. They see God as acting within the stream of human history, a stream with the Genesis narrative as its source and the vision of Revelation as its fullness. A deliberate beginning leads to a planned conclusion through years of controlled (but not fatalistically determined) centuries. You and I stand in that stream of history, in the centre of God's purposes. And while we find that hard enough to comprehend, Genesis tells us that those purposes also embrace the whole of creation, and not man alone.

People, plastic and potatoes

It was raining lightly as the dog and I walked across the fields and through the woods this evening. The warm, sweet smell of damp undergrowth seemed more ravishing although less refined than the scents wafting up from the perfume factory at the bottom of the hill. The chorus of birdsong that erupted from the trees as the rain ceased did not rival Handel's *Messiah* for harmony, yet it contained that inimitable note of spontaneous gaiety one usually associates with carefree lovers.

Man has always felt an essential unity with nature; he has, after all, spent the largest proportion of his history in close association with it. It is only within the last hundred years that the majority of westerners have lived beyond sight of sheep and smell of sow, breeding children for whom such creatures seem almost as mythical as Doctor Doolittle's colourful menagerie. Acres of tarmac have hidden the soil from our eyes; tower blocks have replaced trees as the dominant features of the landscape, and the songs of birds and snorts of pigs have given way to the roar of traffic. Passing down the rows of colourful cartons on supermarket shelves it is easy to forget that we still depend entirely upon the earth for everything we use, plastic containers included.

The suburban garden and the safari park (where we are enjoined to see wild animals in their 'natural' setting) remain eloquent testimonies to the fact that man's need to be close to green and living things has not disappeared. Renes Dubos, a biologist, comments:

> Air, water, soil, and fire, the rhythms of nature and the variety of living things, are not of interest only as chemical mixtures, physical forces, or biological phenomena; they are the very influences that have shaped human life and thereby created deep human needs that will not change.[5]

This is fully in accord with the biblical view of man. We are constituted of the same chemical components as the rest of creation (Genesis 2:7) and we rely on the products of the earth for physical life. 'Thou dost cause the grass to grow for the cattle, and plants for man to cultivate, that he may bring forth food from the earth, and wine to gladden the heart of man, oil to make his face shine, and bread to strengthen man's heart' (Psalm 104:14). Man is a cultivator, not a collector; in the creation narrative he is given the responsibility of caring for the physical environment and developing its resources. He is given 'dominion' over everything else; he is God's deputy ruler in the world (Genesis 1:28).

The fact that authority and identification are complementary is illustrated by the naming of the animals (Genesis 2:18ff.); name-giving assumes authority, the search for a helper among the animals implies a close identification with them. Man's dominion was never intended, however, to become the domination which has produced the pile-up of pollution and the exhaustion of resources rivalling wars and rumours of wars for a place in the press. The biblical command is not 'Exploit!'; rather it is a caution, 'Enough!'

> Perhaps the most urgent task that faces us in this century is to see and feel the fact of our union with nature. The idea that man stands outside nature was part of the old romantic delusion of

both religion and science . . . Alienation is the great disorder of modern man.[6]

The solution to that alienation is not to be found simply in renouncing industrialism and in returning to the simple life of yesteryear. Rather, the solution lies in discovering and treating the *causes* of the alienation which, in fact, is not the disorder of modern man alone. It has been evident in every generation, and is related to man's personal alienation from the Creator of all things. And that is the subject of one of the most misunderstood words of the Bible, 'sin'.

Follow-up

1. What does Psalm 104 teach about God's relationship to the physical order? (See also Psalms 19:1–4; 33:6–9; Jeremiah 10:11–13; Colossians 1:16–20; Hebrews 11:3.)
2. What does Isaiah 40:21–31 tell us about the Creator's relationship with man? (See also Isaiah 42:5; Amos 4:13; 2 Corinthians 5:17.)
3. How does the Bible regard the historicity of Adam? (See Isaiah 43:27; Luke 3:38; Romans 5:12, 14; 1 Corinthians 11:8; 15:21f., 45; 2 Corinthians 11:3; 1 Timothy 2:13.)

References

[1] W. R. Bowie, *The interpreter's Bible* (New York: Abingdon Press, 1952), p. 467.
[2] Advertisement for the British Humanist Association in *The new humanist*, June 1974.
[3] J. D. Bernal, *The origin of life* (Weidenfeld and Nicolson, 1967), p. 140.
[4] David Gascoyne, 'Fragments towards a *religio poetae*', *Collected poems* (Oxford University Press, 1965).

[5] Rene Dubos, *So human an animal* (Hart-Davies, 1970), p. 160.

[6] J. Lewis and B. Towers, *Naked ape or homo sapiens?* (Garnstone Press, 1972), p. 46.

'*Man is an exception, whatever else he is ... If it is not true that a divine being fell, then we can only say that one of the animals went entirely off its head.*'
(G. K. Chesterton)

'*Forgive the world: they are all fools.*'
(Seneca)

2

The tragedy of mankind

'Be sure your sin will find you out' rivals 'The end is nigh' for a place on the placards of cartoon Christians. Sin has been labelled 'the Christian neurosis', the preoccupation of dull people who in their drab buildings practise a dismal religion offering penitential prayers to an implacable God. It is a subject too morose, too remote, for 'enlightened' people in this day and age.

Yet behind the flashing neon lights of the big city, a pocket is picked, a girl is raped and a petty criminal stabbed. Somewhere a train is wrecked by the soccer fans it carries home. Violence stalks the streets of every nation and is no longer restricted to the organized battles of king and country. The emotional shock-waves of Hiroshima still reverberate around a globe which has apparently recovered physically from the atomic blast that devastated thousands of square miles and earned the epitaph 'the tragedy of mankind'.[1]

Something certainly is wrong with the world; sin is not a concept entirely divorced from reality. With the phenomenal expansion of technology and education has come blow after blow of wickedness and aggression. Mankind stands dazed, uncertain of the way ahead, and unable to discover the causes of the problem, let alone the answers. No society has ever fully succeeded in eradicating the evils which stare from the headlines of our morning papers; indeed, there is evidence to suggest that 'prehistoric man was, on the whole, a more peace-

27

ful, co-operative, unwarlike unaggressive creature than we are'.[2]

It is tempting to stand apart from this dark face of human nature as if it had nothing to do with us personally. C. S. Lewis, however, points out that 'those who do not think about their own sins make up for it by thinking incessantly about the sins of others'.[3] In a famous correspondence in *The Times* on what was wrong with the world, G. K. Chesterton wrote simply, 'Sir, I am.' It is at this personal level that the Bible begins to deal with the tragedy of mankind.

'Surely', says the author of Ecclesiastes, 'there is not a righteous man on earth who does good and never sins' (7:20). John the apostle is less polite: 'If we say we have no sin, we deceive ourselves, and the truth is not in us' (1 John 1:8). John the Baptist and his cousin Jesus Christ both declared at the outset of their ministries that they came to preach repentance to sinners (Mark 1:4; Luke 5:32) and that no-one was excluded from this category.

The Bible is like a mirror, faithfully reflecting the vices as well as the virtues of its characters and its readers. If, like the Queen in the story of Snow White, we look into it conscious of our comparative purity and ask, 'Mirror, mirror on the wall, who is the fairest of them all?' the reply always comes, 'Not you, for a start!' In our most honest moments, we know that 'the lust of the flesh and the lust of the eyes and the pride of life' (1 John 2:16) are not restricted to criminals and despots. Materialism, greed and arrogance perform on life's stage wearing a variety of innocuous masks.

To understand the character of man's sinfulness we must return to Adam and Eve. In their experience we discover its basic cause, and we are given a brief summary of the biblical concept of sin.

In the beginning

Poetic imagination has often portrayed the garden in Eden as a kind of weedless Camelot where it rained only at night. No doubt it was a very beautiful place; but all we are told about the scenery is that the trees were 'pleasant to the sight and good for food' (Genesis 2:9). The narrative does not concern us with trivial (although interesting) details; it explains two more important truths within its historical framework.

First, Eden is a place where God's presence is recognized and welcomed. He is the resident landlord who has provided a comfortable home for his tenant, and who has given conditions for the tenure of the property: 'You may freely eat of every tree of the garden; but of the tree of the knowledge of good and evil you shall not eat, for in the day that you eat of it you shall die' (Genesis 2:16f.).

'Typical of God,' I hear someone say. 'He's always putting some "Thou shalt not" damper on our freedom.' The Bible gives several reasons for God's law. It is an expression of the moral character of 'the Father of lights with whom there is no variation or shadow due to change' (James 1:17). It teaches men the nature and extent of sin: 'I should not have known what sin was except for the Law,' explains Paul (Romans 7:7, Jerusalem Bible). It provides a guide to the way God intended the universe to operate; like a manufacturer's handbook it shows what should and should not be done if his product is to function smoothly.

The threat of punishment which accompanies God's law is not intended to convey the impression that he is a slave-owner, whip in hand, ready to pounce on the slightest slip; it expresses his moral righteousness. The word 'righteous' means 'right acting'; the perfect law-giver cannot compromise himself. Justice must always be done, and not only when *we* feel there is an exceptionally deserving case. The God who is 'light' and in whom is 'no darkness at all' (1 John 1:5) must punish both the murderer of an innocent child, and the gossip who murders the half-innocent reputation of an enemy. Light cannot co-exist with the slightest trace of darkness; harmony and discord are incompatible; moral perfection and moral rejection are abhorrent to one another.

The second important truth in the garden of Eden story is that the people God created were themselves morally perfect, for a while. 'God made man upright, but they have sought out many devices' (Ecclesiastes 7:29). One of the greatest theological battles in church history was fought over this, and the dust has not yet settled. A British monk named Pelagius, towards the end of the fourth century, declared that Adam was created not morally *upright*, but morally *neutral*. Within Adam's free choice, he alleged, lay his future destiny: if he chose to obey he could become perfect; if he chose to disobey he would become sinful.

It was not, however, as if God took a complete novice, sat him for the first time behind the controls of a car, gave him no driving lessons, and told him to pass his test first time in a busy city centre. Rather, he put at the steering-wheel of his world a creature who was trained and equipped to deal successfully with any emergency situation. Adam's action was to drive deliberately into the wall. That is why Genesis 3 is often headed 'the fall'; the entry of sin into the world was no accident or mistake but the wilful action of a person who turned his back on all that he knew to be right and true. When Paul writes, 'Adam was not deceived, but the woman was deceived and became a transgressor' (1 Timothy 2:14), he was not exhibiting the male chauvinist streak he is often (wrongly) accused of. He is emphasizing that Adam knew exactly what he was doing, even if Eve did not see all the issues so clearly.

Just how the tempter came to be in the garden is not ex-plained. The temptation itself was certainly not a remnant of a pre-human instinct in Adam; nor was it the action of God, who

30

'cannot be tempted with evil' and who 'tempts no one' (James 1:13). There are occasional hints in Scripture of a rebellion by spiritual beings, but there is no question of an eternal, unresolved dual between an uncontrollable evil and an immovable good. Satan is treated as a personal force to be reckoned with, but he is a trespasser and an intruder; he has no legal right of entry into the world; he has forced his way in to steal the power and the glory that belong to God. And, as Luther quaintly put it, 'his doom is writ'; the sentence of death has been passed, and the execution is timed for what John calls 'the second death' after the return of Jesus to the world (Revelation 20:14; 21:8). In the meantime, you and I have the promise that we can be 'more than conquerors through him who loved us' (Romans 8:37) as, like Adam and Eve, we face the skirmishes and the temptations for ourselves.

The end of the beginning

It came, as temptations always come, from an unexpected quarter and in a deceptive manner. 'Now the serpent was more subtle (or shrewd) than any other wild creature.' The command of God was questioned, '*Did* God say, "You shall not eat . . . "?' and then distorted, ' "of *any* tree of the garden?" ' Eve lacked assurance and she was given the assertion, 'You will not die.' Her vanity was touched by the advertisement copy, 'Your eyes will be opened, and you will be like God, knowing good and evil.' She silenced the internal conflict by a rationalization; 'The tree was good for food, and . . . a delight to the eyes, and . . . to be desired to make one wise.' All that was left for her to do was to taste the fruit and give Adam a bite as well (Genesis 3:1–6).

We have already noticed that Adam, at least, acted deliberately, knowing that this seemingly minor action was fundamentally wrong. This is the essence of sin: 'Every one who commits sin is guilty of lawlessness; sin is lawlessness' (1 John 3:4). To reject the command, which expresses the character of God, is to reject God himself.

Jesus illustrated this in his parable of the prodigal son (Luke 15:11–32). The younger son of the family cashes the inheritance which would normally have come to him upon his father's death. He spends it as he chooses without reference to the father's wishes, and with no apparent concern for the future of the family. The elder son, having remained loyal to the needs of the family estate, shows a similar disregard for the father's wishes when his brother returns. In the scale of values of his hard business world, there is no place for the love and forgiveness of the father.

Sin is living without reference to the wishes of God. 'It is the dare of God's justice, the rape of his mercy, the jeer of his patience, the slight of his power, the contempt of his love.'[4] Expressed in actions or omissions which vary from violence and aggression to envy and self-centredness, our sin is primarily an attitude of rebellion towards, or forgetfulness of, God himself.

It was not, therefore, a twisting of the facts when noble king David, after an ignoble double-act of murder and adultery, confessed to God, 'Against thee, thee only, have I sinned' (Psalm 51:4). That was precisely what he had done. Similarly the prodigal son, in his prepared speech for the stony silence he expected on the doorstep, declared, 'Father, I have sinned *against* heaven and *before* you' (Luke 15:18). Paul explains (1 Corinthians 8:12) that to sin against another Christian is to sin against the Lord to whom he belongs.

Jesus viewed sin as a debt to God (Luke 11:4); we have not paid him our respect or given him our love. The essence of sin, he tells his followers shortly before his death, is in refusing to believe in him (John 16:9). Whenever John's Gospel uses the formula 'believe in' it means personal commitment in relationship; the very thing which existed between God and man in the garden before the fall. The core of Christianity is that because of man's irrational desire and impulsive decision to achieve total independence from God and his law ('You will be like God'), the Christ who 'did not count equality with God a thing to be grasped' had to empty himself, 'taking the form of a servant'. Then, in order for the relationship to be restored, he 'became obedient unto death, even death on a cross' (Philippians 2:6–8).

The beginning of the end

'Then the eyes of both were opened, and they knew that they were naked.' Suddenly, they realize they are different; child-like innocence has given place to adult guilt and shame. The promised 'knowledge' has been granted, but they discover too late that the slick salesman has conned them with only an unpleasant first-hand experience of evil. Their reaction is human and predictable: 'The man and his wife hid themselves from the presence of the Lord God' (Genesis 3:7f.). They ran; and ever since that day men and women have fled from the uncomfortable presence of a holy God.

> I fled Him, down the nights and down the days;
> I fled Him, down the arches of the years;
> I fled Him, down the labyrinthine ways
> Of my own mind; and in the mist of tears
> I hid from Him, and under running laughter.[5]

Adam and Eve were never the same again. And nor was the world. God's abhorrence of sin matched their fear of his presence; they were driven from the garden *and no-one else was allowed to approach it* (Genesis 3:24). Eden, the place of God's manifest presence on earth, no longer exists. God, far from 'walking in the garden in the cool of the day' (Genesis 3:8),

3   33

seems to many people to have completely disappeared; 'missing, believed dead'. The way to the source of true humanity and to God himself is barred to you and me because of the sin of one person.

And you will not be the first person to cry, 'That's not fair!' Pelagius expressed what is now a common belief, that *every* person is born his or her own Adam, a neutral being in a neutral world. Just as Adam, however, was not neutral but righteous, so we are not neutral and we most certainly do not live in a morally neutral world. It is shot through with corruption and is centred squarely on man, not God. The tiniest child appears to have a natural bias away from what is good and right, as every parent knows only too well. And grown adults, for all their education, don't appear to be much better; you and I often find ourselves incapable of living up to our own standards, which we usually set far below the standards of God.

The Bible justifies its assertion that we all share in the guilt and subsequent punishment of Adam by appealing to a concept which is unfamiliar to our western ears: corporate solidarity. We saw a little of this in the previous chapter; momentous events leave a lasting impact on culture and conscience. The Bible goes further than this and suggests that an individual's action, however small, affects the rest of society. A tiny pebble thrown into a lake will change the whole face of the water. Mankind is held together in a unified mass like the molecules of water combining to form the lake; one action will send ripples all the way across. Albert Camus' novel *The plague* is a parable about the ills of modern society. One of the characters confesses his share in the problem:

I came to understand that I, anyhow, had had plague through all these long years in which, paradoxically enough, I'd believed with all my soul that I was fighting it. I learned that I had had an indirect hand in the deaths of thousands of people; that I'd even

34

approved their deaths by approving of acts and principles which could only end that way.[6]

We shape the future of ourselves and others by our present deeds that are themselves based on past decisions; if that is true for us, how much more for the first man who sinned?

Furthermore, Adam is viewed in Scripture as the head of the race, the chosen representative who is responsible for making decisions on behalf of others. The concept is familiar: if David kills Goliath, the Philistine army will be defeated; when a head of state declares war everyone is involved, including those who disapprove of his decision and who did not vote for him; the Olympic record-breaker wins not only a gold medal for himself, but honour for his country. Moreover, these events have repercussions not only in the lifetime of those concerned, but they change the course of history. The solidarity of the race, sometimes (and usually sentimentally) called 'the brotherhood of man', weaves the various threads of humanity into a single fabric.

The end of these things . . .

'Why all this talk about hell in the hereafter?' a neighbour of mine once asked. 'I think this world is hell enough.' He was right, up to a point; hell is the absence of God, a vacuum of truth and goodness, a negation of life. To be born a human being is to be born into a hell of barrenness; conceived under the curse, weaned in the wilderness beyond Eden. 'I feel as if I had died already and am now living a posthumous existence,' exclaimed the poet Keats.[7] That is the *real* tragedy of mankind.

'The end of those things is death' (Romans 6:21). 'In the day that you eat of it you shall die' (Genesis 2:17). But Adam did not die; at least, not immediately. Either God ate his words the moment Adam's teeth sank into the fruit, or else the Bible puts a different meaning on the word 'death'.

The word is in fact used to describe the separation from God which we have already noted, and of which physical death is but a small part. 'Your iniquities have made a separation between you and your God,' writes Isaiah, 'and your sins have hid his face from you' (Isaiah 59:2). Paul agrees: 'You were dead through the trespasses and sins in which you once walked . . . at that time separated from Christ . . . having no hope and without God in the world' (Ephesians 2:1f., 12). How this death features in our daily experience will be seen as we examine the other aspects of our humanity, and by the end of this book we shall see that the theologians have considerable justification for using the phrase 'total depravity'. By it they do not mean that every person is as bad as they possibly can be; rather, they mean that every area of man's personality is tainted by the consequences of being banished from Eden and alienated from its Creator.

One of these consequences is that man is totally incapable of 'making up' with God and getting back into a close relationship of harmony with him. All the religious systems of the world, cut and trimmed to suit every human convenience and culture, cannot bring us one little bit closer to him. That relationship demands total moral righteousness, and no amount of sacrifice, singing or social service can create it. The abyss is too deep to be scaled; the chasm too broad to be spanned. The sentry at the gate is under orders to admit no-one, and he cannot be bribed.

It follows that the noblest life or the most heroic deed cannot of itself turn a sinner into a saint. 'Those who are in the flesh cannot please God,' writes Paul (Romans 8:8). 'We have all become like one who is unclean,' agrees Isaiah, 'and all our righteous deeds are like a polluted garment' (Isaiah 64:6). The English translation is euphemistic; the 'polluted garment' is literally 'the rags of a menstruous woman', and the revulsion is intentional. Jesus was no less emphatic; 'He who commits sin is a slave to sin,' he said (John 8:34), and in the sermon on the mount he made it clear that a bad tree cannot bear good fruit (Matthew 7:18).

These statements underline the fact that human nature as we now know it is but a poor reflection of what it should be; they do not delete personal responsibility from the balance-sheet. They teach the corruption of man; they do not deny his accountability. 'Temptations to sin are sure to come,' said Jesus, *but woe to him by whom they come!*' (Luke 17:1). These are not doom-laden texts emptied of hope. Christianity is a message of good news, a promise of renewal. The sentry *will* unlock the gate; but only on the special orders of the King who himself has fulfilled the conditions for entry. The abyss *will* be scaled and the chasm spanned, but by the wisdom and work of God, not man. At times we fail to take seriously the corruption of human nature and the heinousness of sin. This has led at times not to a religion of hope but to an emaciated Christianity which does not impress the sceptic and which produces believers whose superficiality is seen by all except themselves.

A further consequence of our alienation from God is the hideous delusion that such a state of affairs is normal. Standards are reversed under the pretext of progress, but we cannot perceive that our movement is backwards. Sin is swept under the carpet like so much fluff, and we convince ourselves that the resulting bulge adds to the décor. We are blind men fooling ourselves that darkness is light, that blindness is sight. 'For you say, I am rich, I have prospered, and I need nothing; not knowing that you are wretched, pitiable, poor, blind, and naked' (Revelation 3:17). To bleat that it is unfair to expect us to see when we cannot help being blind only proves our blindness; once upon a time there lived a man who offered sight to the blind, but we nailed him to a cross. The Light hurt our eyes too much.

This blindness of fallen man was brought home to me when I read of the madness of Vaslav Nijinksy. He was a dancer with the Russian Ballet whose sensational abilities stunned the world of the early 1900s. When he was twenty-nine years old, at the peak of his career, he was declared incurably insane, and he never danced again. This is how his friends described his condition: 'a blind man, calm and absent'; 'a human being who is not of this world ... who knows nothing'; 'perfectly happy, just as he was, sunk in his eternal dream'.[8] Happy, perhaps, but like our hedonistic culture, totally divorced from true reality.

Martin Luther once described fallen human nature as 'the self that is bent back on itself'.[9] We exhibit the characteristics of madmen; we tear down established structures and tread values under foot for no other reason than that we have grown tired of them. We enclose ourselves within the narrow confines of materialism and like caged birds flutter (because we cannot fly) from one corner to another in a vain search for the life that could never be contained there. Other people, if we notice them at all, become objects to be held at a distance lest they interfere with our self-oriented march to we know not where. Man has displaced God from the centre of his attentions, seized the throne, and passes the time paying homage to himself.

Even nature has been affected by human fallenness. It is not simply that human greed has created an ecological crisis, killed Lake Erie and contaminated the environment. The very unity man once had with nature has been broken; the internal unity of nature herself has been ruptured and she runs wild. 'Cursed is the ground because of you' (Genesis 3:17); 'Therefore the land mourns, and all who dwell in it languish, and also the beasts of the field, and the birds of the air; and even the fish of the sea are taken away' (Hosea 4:3).

'The wages of sin is death' (Romans 6:23); we are the dead,

you and I, and we live in a dying world. Not the world of *maya*, the illusion spoken of by the orientals, though; there is still much within life that is rich and real. It is still God's world, we are still God's creatures, and the Bible never speaks of the death which is alienation from God without speaking of the life which is reconciliation to him. Paul continues, '... but the free gift of God is eternal life in Christ Jesus our Lord.' This life is much more than the kind of life philosopher John MacMurray described—

> devastatingly mean and poverty stricken and ridiculous; ... whatever the reality of human life may be, the kind of life we live in Europe in the twentieth century is a fantastic travesty of it. In our ways of living we have certainly not grasped the significance of life ... We cannot escape from the negative character of the life we all live together. Nor do we know how to live otherwise.[10]

We do not always conceive of modern life in such pessimistic terms. Nor do we usually plumb the depths of despair of the girl who, because she was so unsure of her identity that she doubted if she was human, slashed her wrists to see if there was any blood in her body.[11] That doesn't necessarily mean that MacMurray's picture is false or that the girl was mentally deranged. Perhaps it is that our conception of life is too narrow, or that we have never asked the fundamental questions which were on the girl's mind.

I wonder if you would be able to give a coherent answer to the question, 'Who am I? What does being human really consist of?' Let me introduce you to someone else who asked these questions, and to the answers the Bible gives.

Follow-up

1. Look up the following verses; what do they tell you about the character of sin? Leviticus 19:17; Deuteronomy 9:18; 1

Samuel 15:23; Psalms 14:3; 51:5; Jeremiah 44:23; Romans 1:29ff.; Hebrews 3:13; 12:1; James 1:15; 2:9; 4:17; 1 John 5:16.

2. What does the Bible have to say about the origin of evil? See Isaiah 14:12–21 and Ezekiel 28:11–19. These prophecies are about human rulers, but their language suggests much more, and they have traditionally been taken as allegories of the fall of Satan. See also John 8:44; 1 Timothy 3:6; 1 John 3:8; Jude 6; and compare Jeremiah 17:9; Mark 7:20–23.

3. What are the causes and cures of temptation? 1 Chronicles 21:1, 7f.; Matthew 4:1–11; 1 Corinthians 10:12f.; James 1:13–15; 1 Peter 5:6–9; 1 John 1:9—2:3.

References

[1] Leo Szilard, quoted by J. Bronowski, *The ascent of man* (BBC Publications, 1973), p. 370.

[2] J. Lewis and B. Towers, *Naked ape or homo sapiens?* (Garnstone Press, 1972), pp. 63f.

[3] C. S. Lewis, *Undeceptions* (Bles, 1971), p. 95.

[4] Ralph Venning, *The plague of plagues* (Banner of Truth, 1965), p. 32.

[5] Francis Thomson, 'The Hound of Heaven', *Selected poems of Francis Thomson* (Jonathan Cape, 1929), p. 49.

[6] Albert Camus, *The plague* (Hamish Hamilton, 1948), p. 233.

[7] Quoted by Colin Wilson, *The outsider* (Gollancz, 1970), p. 15.

[8] Françoise Reiss, *Nijinsky: a biography* (A. and C. Black, 1960), pp. 189, 190, 195.

[9] Quoted by Emil Brunner, *Man in revolt* (Lutterworth Press, 1939), p. 136.

[10] John MacMurray, *Reason and emotion* (Faber, 1972), p. 58.

[11] Cited by Erich Fromm, *The anatomy of human destructiveness* (Jonathan Cape, 1974), p. 249.

'He seemed like a walking blasphemy, a blend of the angel and the ape.'
(G. K. Chesterton)

'If I could convince myself that my horse could grasp the concept of "self", I would at once dismount and treat him as my friend.'
(Kant)

3
Between ape and angel

A student in her late teens, she looked at me sheepishly through her long blonde hair, and slowly stirred her coffee.

'I woke up one morning', she began, 'and I realized that I was no longer a girl but a woman. It was all so sudden. It might sound funny to you, but I just didn't know who I was.'

No, it did not sound funny, as we talked over the emotional breakdown from which she was recovering. She was asking directly the question which lies behind the culture and chaos of the twentieth century: 'Who am I?'

Uncomfortable questions have a habit of piercing the comfortable shell of materialism in which most of us dwell. From the privacy of our darkened living-rooms we watch banks being robbed, bombs exploding and babies dying. Next day, as we stand in the bus queue, we ask what the world is coming to, but underneath the question really is, Where, in this threatening world, may we find true, lasting security? An advertisement, 'Computers need people', awakens us to the dehumanizing process which reduces people to numbers, chaining them like slaves to the machinery of our 'civilized' systems. Instinctively we feel that this was not how life was meant to be.

Who was he? ... A white monkey hung far out on a spindly heaventree of stars. A fleck of dust condemned to know it is a fleck of dust. A mouse in a furnace. A smothered scream.[1]

That is how one of John Updike's fictional characters faces

the problem of human identity. 'Then God said, "Let us make man in our image, after our likeness,"' is how the Bible answers it (Genesis 1:26), and immediately other problems loom large.

More than an ape

In 1966, Austrian scientist Konrad Lorenz drove what seemed to be a decisive nail into the coffin in which was buried the popular belief in the uniqueness of man. In his book *On aggression* he drew the already familiar parallel between the behaviour of animals and men, illustrated it from his own painstaking research into animal aggression, and concluded that the 'deepest strata of the human personality are, in their dynamics, not essentially different from the instincts of animals'.[2] The way was open for human beings to be regarded simply as naked apes roaming about in a human zoo.

That human behaviour can resemble that of the animals is something that the Bible is familiar with. People are quite capable of behaving stupidly 'like a horse or a mule' (Psalm 32:9) and they will be wise if they learn about prudence from the ant (Proverbs 6:6). The psalmist likens his enemies to the ravaging dog, the roaring lion and the ruthless oxen which come without cause to destroy him and his property (Psalm 22:20f.), and the prophet draws a parallel between adulterers and 'well-fed lusty stallions, each neighing for his neighbour's wife' (Jeremiah 5:8). Jesus warned that hungry 'wolves' with false teaching or luring temptation would try to snatch his followers like sheep from a pen (John 10:1–30).

Our contemporary language is more vivid. A child monkeys around aping his heroes, whilst an adult who does the same is an ass. Police are sometimes called pigs, and unscrupulous enemies dogs. Women can fight like tigers, behave like bitches, preen themselves like birds and have a whale of a time in hen parties; meanwhile, their menfolk travel packed like sardines in tin trains to the concrete jungle where they compete in the rat race. Coming together at night in their nests, they breed like rabbits and add to the millions who already crawl like ants across the face of the earth.

Konrad Lorenz is certainly not without evidence to support his views; his logic, however, is questionable. To demonstrate that A is like B is not at all the same thing as proving that A *is* B. It is man who puts the animals in zoos and who spies upon their habits, not vice versa. To describe human behaviour in animal terms is nearly always an insult, not a compliment. There is in man a niggling belief that he is totally different from the animal kingdom. One reason for this is the qualitative difference between man's achievements and theirs; the ants have yet to invent accountancy, and chimpanzees have never seen the need for computers. Another reason is given in the Bible: man is made in God's image, the animals are not.

This distinction is all the more striking in the Genesis account of creation because both man and the animal world are made on the same 'day', but it is only man who is described as God's image. The phrase gives a fundamental definition of humanness; it is that which makes you and me different from what is not human. Perhaps our preference to be associated with the animals rather than to be allied to the Almighty is the guilty reaction of a race which has failed to be true to its character.

Less than an angel

The word 'image' is used in the Old Testament for a statue ('You . . . made for yourself images of men': Ezekiel 16:17), and for a picture ('She saw men portrayed upon the wall, the images of the Chaldeans portrayed in vermilion': Ezekiel 23:14). The word 'likeness' is a parallel term meaning 'a resemblance'; Ezekiel saw in a vision 'something that looked

45

like burning coals of fire' (1:13). The biblical conception of man in God's image is not, however, a physical one.

The Greek legend of creation had Prometheus moulding a figure in the shape of the gods, and the Mormons believe that God, because he has appeared in human form, must have a physical body. The Jewish authors of Scripture would be horrified; 'He is not a man' (1 Samuel 15:29); 'God is spirit' (John 4:24).

That God occasionally appears in human form is undeniable. He visited Abraham as a man (Genesis 18) and Jesus Christ claimed to be God in human flesh (John 6:38). Nowhere does the Bible suggest that God is always man-shaped; he 'inhabits eternity' (Isaiah 57:15). Human terms are sometimes used to describe him; when the psalmist wrote, 'The eyes of the Lord are toward the righteous, and his ears toward their cry' (Psalm 34:15) he was using the only concepts available to him to depict God as all-seeing and all-knowing. The poetic symbolism is an approximation pointing beyond itself. The same applies to God's 'emotions'. When he is said to be angry, for instance, he is not being portrayed as a crotchety Creator, a despotic deity or an explosive employer. His anger has nothing to do with human irritability or impatience, but is an almost unimaginable (because wholly just and reasonable) reaction to denials of his holiness and majesty.

God's holiness gives us a clue as to the meaning of his 'image'. Man, made before the fall in the image of God, was intended to reflect his Creator's moral purity; man was a finite representation of God's infinite character. Paul stresses this when writing of the personal life of the Christian: 'Put on the new nature, created after the likeness of God in true righteousness and holiness' (Ephesians 4:24). Being in God's image means we should reflect God, not the animals, in our behaviour: 'You shall be holy, for I am holy' (Leviticus 11:45; 1 Peter 1:16).

Man's banishment from the Eden of God's presence led

some scholars to suggest that the image of God has been lost from human nature. This, however, does not make sense of two things in Scripture. First, there are several references (which we shall see later) to man remaining in God's image *after* the fall. Secondly, the Bible never thinks of a man as *having* the image of God, like a radio or a reputation which he can be given and which he can lose. Rather, man *is* the image of God: 'Let us make man *in* our image.'

In the second century AD, a church leader called Irenaeus suggested that 'image' and 'likeness' were two different aspects of the human personality. 'Image' was the original righteousness lost at the fall, while 'likeness' is the rationality we have retained. The idea has persisted in some form ever since, and of course contains an element of truth; we are still human, and 'there is none righteous, no, not one' (Romans 3:10). During the Reformation in the sixteenth century, however, Luther pointed out that such interpretations cannot be forced on the Hebrew words. He also stressed that the Bible never divides the human personality but always insists on its unity. So how do we reconcile human unrighteousness before God with our remaining in his image?

I once took a photograph of someone who was standing in front of one of those distorting mirrors at the seaside. She has three heads, three legs and a body that looks like a tree trunk about to sprout branches. Yet she is still (just!) recognizable as a human being. You and I are still recognizably human, but far from possessing the kind of humanity God meant us to have. God's image has been grossly distorted.

One of the marks that assures us that we have not sunk to the level of the sub-human is that we instinctively know that there are such things as right and wrong. Our conscience can often be wrong about what is right, and it is not always right about what is wrong; it can be conditioned by many external forces and is by no means an infallible guide to the will of God. None

47

the less, every human being has a conscience, and moral values exist in every human society: 'What the law requires is written on their hearts, while their conscience also bears witness' (Romans 2:15).

In his *Autobiography* G. K. Chesterton recounts how he met a gangster and racketeer in a cafe in Barcelona. The man had written a book about his exploits, but the publishers had stolen most of the royalties. ' "It was a shame," I said sympathetically, "why, it was simply robbery." "I'll say it was," he said with an indignant blow on the table. "It was just plain robbery." '[3] The human moral consciousness exists because it is an aspect of God's image; but it is bent back on the human ego.

It is this moral awareness that makes us accountable to God for our actions even when it is impossible for us ever consistently to live up to his standards. 'Whoever knows what is right to do and fails to do it, for him it is sin' (James 4:17). And coupled with our innate sense of right and wrong is the inescapable religious consciousness of man.

Rather like an elephant . . .

'Why can't I kill God within me?' cries the Knight in Bergman's film *The seventh seal*. 'Why does He live on in this painful and humiliating way even though I curse Him and want to tear Him out of my heart? Why, in spite of everything, is He a baffling reality that I can't shake off?'[4] No man, no tribe or nation has ever succeeded in finally shaking off the conviction that life has a spiritual dimension. Cults may be propagated by commerce, and crimes may have been perpetrated in the name of Christ, but force and finance are totally inadequate to explain the human consciousness of God. Like the proverbial elephant with a prodigious memory, man cannot forget that he is made in the image of a God to whom he can relate.

Paul says that some realization of God's nature is produced

48

by the world around us: 'Ever since the creation of the world his invisible nature, namely, his eternal power and deity, has been clearly perceived in the things that have been made' (Romans 1:20). The author of Ecclesiastes explains the endless quest for God: 'He has put eternity into man's mind; yet so that he cannot find out what God has done from the beginning to the end' (3:11). Augustine summed it up in his famous words, 'Thou hast created us for thyself, and our heart knows no rest until it may repose in thee.'[5]

Man, however, always attempts to cut God down to size; a deity made after the fashion of our own likings and likeness is much more manageable, much less demanding and interfering, than the one 'who sits above the circle of the earth, and its inhabitants are like grasshoppers' (Isaiah 40:22). Paul comments: 'Claiming to be wise, they became fools, and exchanged the glory of the immortal God for images resembling mortal man or birds or animals or reptiles' (Romans 1:22f.).

Our graven images have come a long way from the statues of Apollo and Mars in Athens. Apollo has been given rocket propulsion and sent to patrol a pebble on the shore of a boundless universe. Mars has been covered in milk chocolate and enthroned among the pleasure-gods in a pantheon of affluence. Garden and garage, home and holiday, income and insurance are god-like centres of human attention which have been endowed with honour and glory. An endless procession of ever-new causes have replaced truth and righteousness as the major claims upon our allegiance. But a man-made god is never big enough to satisfy the spiritual desires of humanity, nor finally to silence the eternal God who made us in his image.

When you and I instinctively pray in time of illness or need, when we sense a presence which cannot be described or search for a power that cannot be defined, we are not acting like children nor exhibiting a neurosis. We are beginning to become men. We are still fallen men, of course, and our religious drives

4　　　　　　　　　　49

will not of themselves necessarily propel us to the real God. They could lead us up the popular by-ways of magic, meditation and mysticism. They could send us down the cul-de-sac of pantheistic nature-worship in which hazelnuts, hedgehogs and humans are seen as equal manifestations of an impersonal life-force. They could point to a thousand and one different cults and creeds. But there is only one path which leads to the restoration of the distorted image of God. It is a narrow way, sometimes steep and stony like a mountain track. 'I am the way, and the truth, and the life,' said Jesus; 'no one comes to the Father, but by me' (John 14:6).

. . . or a silver coin . . .

Jesus' controversy with the Pharisees and Herodians over the legitimacy of paying taxes to Rome provides our next clue in the hunt for human identity. Looking at a coin, Jesus asks, 'Whose likeness and inscription is this?' When told it is Caesar's, he comments, 'Render to Caesar the things that are Caesar's, and to God the things that are God's' (Mark 12:13-17).

The word 'likeness' is used elsewhere in the New Testament for the 'image' of God, and the word 'render' literally means 'to pay back a debt'. Jesus is saying that the coin belongs ultimately to Caesar; his image gives it an authenticity and guarantees its value. So it is with man; being stamped with God's image gives us a definite identity and an intrinsic value. Humanity is not any old life, like that of the wilting plant on my desk, to be trodden down or spat upon. It is a special kind of life, made precious by God's mark of worth upon it.

A visitor from another planet, of course, would find that hard to believe. He would see nations on the rampage pouring the blood of their virile young men upon the ground. He would see giant commercial enterprises sweeping little men in corner shops and workshops clean out of house and home like so many beetles being brushed out of dusty corners. And he would see decent-living you and me spending time and money watching actors in fake fights shooting blank bullets and shedding simulated blood, providing imaginative outlets for the greed and hatred we nurse in our hearts; wishing on real people, people in God's image, the worst things possible.

James, blunt as ever, says that with the tongue 'we bless the Lord and Father, and with it we curse men, who are made in the likeness of God . . . My brethren, this ought not to be so' (James 3:9). 'Every one who is angry with his brother (and not only those who kill) shall be liable to judgment,' said Jesus (Matthew 5:21f.). Murder and maliciousness, angry curses and criminal actions, jealousy, hatred and envy, all alike devalue the image of God in which everyone is made. But no-one would think of despising a coin or of rendering it valueless by obliterating the likeness of the head of state.

A little while ago I saw in our village a child being pushed in a wheelchair. He was horribly deformed; tiny hands protruded from his shoulders, and tiny feet were where his thighs should have been. The day before I had travelled on a train in which a mentally deranged man muttered incoherently to everyone in the carriage. His hollow cheeks and unshaven chin, his vacant eyes and ragged clothes, presented a tragic picture of misery and hopelessness. But abnormality does not rob a man of his humanity. He is as much the distorted image of God as you and I; he is still the neighbour to be loved, not kicked or despised, or even merely pitied.

The absolute value of human life is stressed in the story of Noah. God says, 'Whoever sheds the blood of man, by man shall his blood be shed; for God made man in his own image' (Genesis 9:6). That is not a text to justify revenge; it is to prevent revenge becoming a feud. More especially it implies that any punishment less than death for murder within an organized society rates the life of the criminal above that of his victim; human life is so precious that to destroy it is a crime of the utmost seriousness. Alongside that must be placed the story of Cain who murdered his brother in cold blood. God puts a special mark on Cain's forehead, 'lest any who came upon him should kill him' (Genesis 4:15). God is emphasizing that even the most despicable man still possesses his mark, is still in his image and under his care.

Has the incredible truth which topples all our accepted values begun to dawn? Being in God's image gives a sanctity to all human life; it gives dignity to the oppressed and the unfortunate. *It also gives an identical value to the human life of the oppressors and all others who appear socially dangerous.* Which is something to think about.

. . . but not a clockwork orange

Anthony Burgess had something similar to think about in his novel *A clockwork orange*. Alex, the main character, is a violent teenage criminal from a perfectly ordinary home; 'What I do I do because I want to do,' he says.[6] After a spell in gaol, he is put on to a new treatment which makes him ill at the sight or thought of violence. This forces him to act pleasantly even in the face of provocation, and eventually he is pronounced 'cured'. But he has lost his freedom of choice, and as another character in the book comments, 'A man who cannot choose ceases to be a man.'[7] Burgess is asking if we want a society peopled with humans free to choose evil, or with 'clockwork oranges' automatically producing the correct social responses.

The ability to make considered decisions marks man off from both beast and machine, and has often been seen as an effect of being made in God's image. Unlike the animals, we do not have to act according to the promptings of pain or pleasure; we can endure pain or forgo pleasure willingly because of moral or other factors which we consider to be more important. Our reactions are not merely 'programmed' responses, because under certain circumstances we refuse or fail to do what we believe we should: 'I do not do the good I want, but the evil I do not want is what I do' (Romans 7:19).

Of course, at times we act instinctively, and our brains do have certain similarities to computers, but we have something which neither animals nor machines can have, and that is 'personhood'. A creature that can think abstractly and communicate ideas rationally, feel emotionally and be fully conscious of itself as a unique being, act selfishly or on the basis of principle and not of necessity, and which above all can enter into a relationship of love and service with God and others – this we call a person. God, who is personal in that he is more-than-human and not an impersonal life force, treats us as persons.

'Choose this day whom you will serve' (Joshua 24:15); a straight choice between heathen superstition or the living God. 'Come to me, all who labour and are heavy laden, and I will give you rest' (Matthew 11:28); an invitation which need not be accepted. 'You shall love the Lord your God with all your heart, and with all your soul, and with all your mind, and with all your strength ... you shall love your neighbour as yourself' (Mark 12:30f.); the total self-giving of love is meaningless if it is a compulsion and not a willing, considered response.*

The Bible often uses the relationship of a father to his son to illustrate this aspect of our humanity. 'When God created man, he made him in the likeness of God ... Adam ... became the father of a son in his own likeness, after his image' (Genesis 5:1, 3). Adam's son Seth, like any man's child, inherits his father's essential nature, his fallen humanness, and perhaps also some similarities of build or personality. These inherited characteristics enable the child to acquire certain

* The Bible also speaks of a serious limitation in the ability of fallen man to choose to love and serve God. We will discuss this later in chapter 9.

others, such as the skills of reading and rowing, qualities like truthfulness, and interests such as stamp collecting. Personal relationships can be built up between people because they share a common human nature which other things like dogs and desks do not possess.

We inherit from God a 'god-likeness' which encompasses our moral responsibility, ability to reason and worship, and so on. He desires that our likeness to him should grow through our relationship to him, as a child's humanity develops through his relationship to his parents. 'Through God you are no longer a slave but a son, and if a son then an heir' (Galatians 4:7). 'Therefore be imitators of God, as beloved children' (Ephesians 5:1). That growth is to continue until the day 'when he appears (and) we shall be like him, for we shall see him as he is' (1 John 3:2). On that day the image of God will be restored, to be seen at last in the richness of its true colours.

That will also be the resurrection day when, according to Jesus, 'they neither marry nor are given in marriage' (Matthew 22:30). To some that may make heaven seem a rather dull and colourless place; to others, the news may come somewhat as a relief! But whatever the future, the battle of the sexes, striving to assert their separate identities while at the same time being deeply aware of their interdependence, continues in the present. 'So God created man in his own image, in the image of God he created him; *male and female he created them*' (Genesis 1:27). From defining our human identity we move on to discuss our human sexuality.

Follow-up

1. Read Psalm 8. What does it have to say about the character of God, and man?
2. What do you know of the character of the God which we should reflect as human beings created in his image? See

Deuteronomy 7:9–11; John 15:12–14; I Peter 2:21–23.

3. What does the New Testament teach about our relationship to God as children of a Father? See Luke 6:35; John 1:12f.; Romans 8:15–17, 23; 2 Corinthians 6:16–18; Galatians 3:26; 4:4–7; Ephesians 1:5; 2:3; 5:8; I John 3:1–3; *cf*. Isaiah 43:6.

4. Man's 'dominion' in the world, his moral consciousness and his capacity for rational decision all add up to *moral responsibility*. Read Mark 14:10f., 17–21, 41–50; *cf*. 13:21–30, and discuss how this applied to Judas. It might be helpful if you also read the accounts in Matthew 26 and Luke 22.

References

[1] John Updike, *Bech: a book* (Andre Deutsch, 1965), p. 124.

[2] Konrad Lorenz, *On aggression* (Methuen, 1966), p. 214.

[3] G. K. Chesterton, *Autobiography* (Hutchinson, 1969), p. 316.

[4] Ingmar Bergman, *The seventh seal* (Lorrimer Publishing, 1968), p. 28.

[5] Augustine, *The confessions of St Augustine* (Fontana, 1957), p. 31.

[6] Anthony Burgess, *A clockwork orange* (Heinemann, 1962), p. 40.

[7] *Op. cit*, p. 161.

'It may be conceded to the mathematicians that four is twice two. But two is not twice one; two is two thousand times one. That is why, in spite of a hundred disadvantages, the world will always return to monogamy.'
(G. K. Chesterton)

'The Girl . . . is the omnipresent icon of consumer society.'
(Harvey Cox)

4
Two of a kind

The Greeks had stories for most things, and the origin of human sexuality was no exception. People, they said, were created bisexual beings with two heads, four arms, and so on. When they grew proud and attempted to oust the gods from heaven, Zeus, the chief of the gods, cut them in half as a punishment. From that moment, every individual was doomed to go through life nursing unfulfilled desires until he or she is re-united with their other half.

The story has unfortunately worked its way into the pop philosophy of the modern world. People still speak of their 'other half', and imply that until marriage, or sexual experience, an individual is somehow incomplete. The Bible will have none of this; the most complete man who ever lived, Jesus of Nazareth, neither married nor had sexual relations with a woman. But he had many friends who were women, and it is at the social level, rather than the sexual level, that the Bible begins its often grossly misunderstood teaching about men and women.

Liberty, equality and fraternity

To many of us, the war-cry of the French Revolution would hardly seem an apt description of the Christian attitude to women. More suitable, we would imagine, is the title of a book published in Leipzig at the end of the sixteenth century: *Women are not human beings*. But that, however, is just the

57

opposite of the assessment made by the author of Genesis: 'God created man in his own image . . . male and female he created them' (1:27).

Equality is stressed here. Even though the orthodox Jew in Jesus' day would daily thank God that he was born neither a Gentile nor a woman, the Scriptures teach that both sexes are equal in status by virtue of being made in the image of God. Paul stresses this in a letter he wrote to a church which was being upset by teachers who wanted to impose Jewish nationalism and discrimination on Gentile converts. 'There is neither Jew nor Greek' within the church, he says, 'there is neither slave nor free, *there is neither male nor female*; for you are all one in Christ Jesus' (Galatians 3:28). In other words, God deals with us not according to our race, sex or social status, but according to our common humanity, even though you and I do not always follow his example.

Now Paul was far from being the misogynist that he is frequently made out to be; his teaching on women was as revolutionary in his day as his charge to masters to treat their slaves as humans and not as dogs. He encouraged the early Christians to show respect and care for women on a scale that a contemporary Roman would have considered at best unnecessary and at worst quite contrary to nature. Widows, instead of being left to beg, were to be provided for by the church (1 Timothy 5:3-16). Husbands, who if they wished could under current Jewish law divorce their wives for such trivial causes as burning their breakfast, were told to love and serve them (Ephesians 5:25).

Turning through the rest of the scriptural record we find that women are by no means excluded from the halls of fame. The forthright leadership of Deborah and the gentle loyalty of Ruth, the courage of Rahab the prostitute and the cruelty of Jezebel the queen – they, like the men, are exposed to posterity for us to learn from, and no judgment is passed on them except concerning the *quality* of their actions. It was the Marys and Marthas who had the temerity to stand by Jesus in his death when his close male companions had forsaken him, and who in his life had 'followed Jesus from Galilee, ministering to him' (Matthew 27:55). And it is in that little aside that the clue to the Christian attitude to the women's liberation movements of our own day lies. Those women did for Jesus what they were best able to do.

The Bible does not advocate *discrimination* on the grounds of sex. It is therefore something of a pity that Christians did not apply the principle of equality within society with the same evangelical fervour as was displayed by the campaigners for factory reform and the emancipation of slaves and children in the nineteenth century. But that apart, the Bible does suggest that there are appropriate *differences of role* for men and women. Equality of status is not at all the same thing as interchangeability of roles. Legislation such as the British Sex Discrimination Act may technically provide for women to become bricklayers and men to become bunny-persons, but it will never be able to change the natural inclinations and abilities of either sex.

It is partly a matter of physical differences, of course. Male and female bodies differ not only in the sexual organs; their whole structures vary. Men are generally broader in the shoulder and narrower in the hip; a woman's shape is determined by fatty tissue and a man's by muscular tissue. She has a smaller skull (but not necessarily an inferior brain!) and a wider pelvis; his legs tend to bow while hers tend to bend inwards. So the man is usually better equipped for building the house, while the woman, physically and psychologically, is more able than him to beautify it. Her body is structured for the function of childbearing, and while no-one would want to relegate the female of the species into the dehumanized role of a battery hen, it is idle to ignore the fact that *generally speaking* a woman finds her greatest (but not necessarily her only) ful-filment in her family life.

To explain this in terms of social conditioning is to fly in the face of the fact that men and women differ in their whole approach to life. The woman tends to be more sensitive and subjective, less analytical and aggressive. Jackie Stewart, world champion racing driver, saw this clearly when he said that 'technically, there is no reason why a woman shouldn't be a Formula One racing driver; emotionally there might be'.[1] It can also be argued that this is precisely what Paul had in mind when he declared that women were not 'to teach or to have authority over men' within the church (1 Timothy 2:12). He never denied that they could exercise a valid and God-inspired ministry; he is suggesting that feminine (and masculine) psychologies are such that spiritual authority and oversight of a fellowship is properly the responsibility of the men. But while that debate goes on into the early hours of tomorrow morning, it is important to remember that cruel jokes, culpable insensitivity bred from ignorance, and the current unisex vogue in fashions have not helped matters. Deliberately to ignore or suppress the rich variations in God's creation is a course of action which can never lead to human liberation.

And it is *liberty* which has been at the heart of Women's Rights movements ever since Mary Wollstonecraft in the eighteenth century derided the feeble educational oppor-tunities offered to her female contemporaries. She saw in her society a system which condemned even the most intelligent of women to remain 'servile dolls fit only to be the playthings of lecherous men'. Where equality of status is recognized, liberty in action should result: freedom implies, among other things, the freedom to be oneself, as a man or a woman.

But one of the consequences of the fall is that human beings frequently *feel* trapped and enslaved, even if they are technically free. They are hemmed in by their own rationality, and their minds lack the eternal dimensions necessary to comprehend reality in its fullness. We are enclosed in our own tents of self-sufficiency, and, terrified that others will slash the canvas and expose us to the difficult demands of selfless relationships, we champion our own cause and neglect that of others. There is no doubt that the male fear of female dominion led to the total banishment of women from pubs and politics, and that that fear is still expressed today when women are banished from the role of partner to that of pin-up.

In Genesis before the fall, Adam and Eve are portrayed as living in a harmony which transcends their separate roles. Adam bears responsibility and authority (which is implied in his giving of names both to the animals and to Eve herself) but he does not in any way dominate her. The domination comes later: Eve is told by God, 'Your desire shall be for your husband, and he shall rule over you' (Genesis 3:16). Her desire for love and protection will be met by possessiveness and over-lording. Eve, having fallen into temptation before Adam, feels for the first time that she is his inferior; and in tempting him she discovers that she has succeeded only in arousing his aggression. The battle of the sexes has begun.

And it is not likely to end until we have learnt to accept ourselves with the limitations with which God created us. In his teaching on marriage relationships, Paul encourages couples to accept their individual roles and to discover in them a new dimension of love. 'The husband is the head of the wife' – caring, protecting, loving and giving – in the same manner as 'Christ is the head of the church' (Ephesians 5:23f.). Our fallen-ness sometimes forbids us to admit that the desire of a woman to be loved is natural, and that the desire of a man to care for her is equally natural. But that brings us to *fraternity*.

Paul states the obvious when he reminds us that 'woman is not independent of man nor man of woman' (1 Corinthians 11:11). In Genesis, Eve's *raison d'être* is to be 'a helper fit' (*i.e.*

suited) for Adam (2:18). She is not to be a slave but a companion; not subsidiary to a master but complementary to a friend. It only takes a visit to a single-sex institution such as a school or a college to remind us that if a healthy culture and community is to develop, we need the specific contributions of both sexes.

It is through love and mutual respect that this companionship is best expressed. The Greeks have at least partially atoned for their misleading story by providing us with four words to describe the rich varieties of love. Friendship, family affection, sensual *eros* and sacrificing *agapē* are widely different manifestations of that most human of all emotions. Each has its place; one of the ironic results of women's lib is that men have been given an excellent excuse (equality) for not bothering with those little tokens of respect towards women that our grandfathers called manners.

The place where love really comes into its own is, of course, in the intimate personal sharing of a couple, and even the sage of old found 'the way of a man with a maiden' too wonderful to begin to understand (Proverbs 30:18f.). But then, love between a man and a woman is too big for words; a hundred and four could scarcely begin to define it. It has a set of values all of its own; 'Many waters cannot quench love, neither can floods drown it. If a man offered for love all the wealth of his house, it would be utterly scorned' (Song of Solomon 8:7). And it has a tantalizing mixture of emotions experienced nowhere else in human life; love, cried Romeo, is

> a madness most discreet,
> A choking gall, and a preserving sweet.[2]

It is hardly surprising therefore that such a complex phenomenon should be counterfeited or cheapened. The desires of *eros* overpower the demands of *agapē*; self-giving turns into self-satisfying. Back-lit figures in colour supplements foster a romantic idealism that conveniently excludes the 'gall' by exaggerating the 'sweet'. Contemporary couples move through a set-piece lovers' dance choreographed by convention, oblivious to the fact that the steps matter less than the spirit which motivates them. But perhaps even they have the edge over those who regard sexual attraction merely as a kind of glandular fever.

Mystery, modesty and maturity

We humans have an unfortunate habit of reacting to extremes by going to their opposites. For instance, it was not so much theological conviction that led the early church to regard sex as evil as an over-reaction to the extreme permissiveness of the contemporary culture. But regard it as evil they did; so Origen, a second-century theologian, castrated himself, and St Augustine in the fourth century declared that the desires he found so hard to come to terms with were the results of the fall. In more recent times, Victorian secrecy has given way to modern naturalism; the element of mystery has been totally removed from sex, thereby lowering it to the level of the bodily functions of eating and evacuating.

The Hebrews were an earthy race; as we shall see in chapter 6, they never despised the body, and sex, like everything else physical, is part of God's good creation. Of course, human sinfulness can distort natural desire into unnatural lasciviousness, and Samson's weakness (for women in general) and David's wilfulness (over Bathsheba in particular) are recorded in Scripture as salutary reminders of the extent of their distortion.

Naturalness is coupled, however, with mystery. Sex is much more to the Bible writers than a temporary physical conjunction of two bodies; it is a permanent union of two personalities. 'A man leaves his father and his mother and cleaves to his wife, and they become one flesh' (Genesis 2:24). 'This mystery', comments Paul, 'is a profound one, and I am saying that it refers to Christ and the church' (Ephesians 5:32). The point of his analogy is that when a person becomes a Christian there is forged a permanent union between him and Jesus Christ. 'You in me and I in you' was how Jesus himself put it (John 14:20), not implying (as some religions would have it) that we are assimilated into the Godhead and thereby lose our personality. Rather, we are brought into a relationship with Jesus which is eternal, which includes a growing awareness of his personal will and character, and which none the less does not violate our freedom and personality.

So with a sexual relationship; it introduces us to a totally new kind of deeply personal *knowledge* of ourselves and our partner. 'Adam knew Eve his wife, and she conceived' (Genesis 4:1) is not a euphemistic way of saying, 'They had intercourse.' It is a shrewd observation of the nature of sex; because our sexuality is not a distinct segment of our humanity, to be joined to another sexually is to be joined physically, emotionally and psychologically. This personal union occurs even in the most casual sexual intercourse. 'Do you not know that he who joins himself to a prostitute becomes one body with her? For, as it is written, "The two shall become one flesh"' (1 Corinthians 6:16).

This is why sexual sin is frowned upon so much in the Bible. It is not that virginity carries any superior spiritual merit, but that chastity (the restriction of sexual activity to the marriage partnership) is a mark of respect for our sexual nature. Casual union with several partners, polygamy (accepted in the Old Testament but never endorsed) and sexual relations with someone of the same sex are not merely transgressions of God's law but also denials of our own humanness (1 Corinthians 6:18). We are just not made to live that way.

Literature is full of examples of the vacuum casual sex can

leave or the conflicts it can create. Solzhenitsyn's Zoya had known the high moments of sexual ecstasy many times, but 'It was never the real thing. It all lacked that stable, deliberate continuity which gives stability to life, indeed gives life itself.'[3] David Gascoyne laments a dead friend in an elegy which sadly concludes,

> the joy
> Of sensual satisfaction seemed so brief, and left
> Only new need.[4]

And John Updike's Foxy tells her lover Piet of the unexpected problems she encountered when she became 'one flesh' with two men in the partner-swapping sub-culture of middle-class America:

I determined to keep you each in place, in watertight compartments. Instead, the two of you are using my body to hold a conversation in. I want to tell you each about the other. I live in fear of calling out the wrong name.[5]

In the face of the mystery of sexual union, the Bible calls for modesty in sexual attitudes and maturity in sexual behaviour. The Shulammite woman, thoroughly immersed in the agony and the ecstasy of sexual love, has the presence of mind to advise her companions not to grab at the promised joy: 'I adjure you, O daughters of Jerusalem, by the gazelles or the hinds of the field, that you stir not up nor awaken love until it please' (Song of Solomon 2:7). The phrase 'until it please' does not mean 'when you like' but 'when the time is ripe'; when the couple, having committed themselves to each other in marriage, are ready to share the very depths of their being; when they have matured to the point where sexual 'knowledge' can spin together as a single thread the strands of self-knowledge they have hitherto revealed to one another.

But you try shouting that from the rooftops, let alone try to practise it. The topless model in the paper smiles, 'Come and get me,' and the tempting air hostess in the advertisement suggests you fly her in soft, gentle comfort. 'The playthings of lecherous men'; times haven't changed much. A man can walk down a main city street on any warm afternoon and he won't need much of an imagination to send the adrenalin coursing through his veins. To say nothing of the bright-eyed salesgirls who aren't really selling you a car or a holiday but a sex symbol or a fantasy. And you hardly notice the bombard-ment of double meanings and coarse suggestions from the family comedy shows that imply that the only thing worth talking about, laughing about, and actually doing, is sex. It's enough to make even Solomon turn in his grave. Is it really any wonder that you and I sometimes find this hard to cope with, and that even those with the best intentions and highest principles occasionally crumble under the pressure, or wilt in the heat?

Brides, babies – and bark?

My host left me alone in the living-room which led into a small summer house overlooking the garden. I wandered out into the summer house, and saw some toys in the corner. A stuffed dog on wheels was sticking out its tongue at a one-eyed teddy bear, and alongside them was parked a pedal car which could have been in a motorway pile-up. It was late afternoon, yet a deathly hush hung over the toys. Where were the laughter and tears, the smiling faces and shouting voices? Slowly I remembered; there were no children any more; they and their mother had left the house; my host was a divorcee. And like ghosts from the past hovering over the rude dog, the blind bear and the dented car, the scenes of family life flashed across my imagination. The young couple absorbed in homemaking, saving and shopping, laying carpets, hanging wallpaper, having fun, being together, now talking excitedly, now quiet and wrapped in wordless love. A child is born, then a second; a difficult pregnancy, perhaps; buckets of nappies; more bills; 'Daddy, mend my doll;' 'Mummy, I've spilt my drink;' not much of a holiday; 'What's the matter with you these days?' 'Will you shut up!'

The ghosts fled as my host returned, but many questions raced in to take their place. 'Till death us do part'; is that realistic or even necessary? Is marriage a divine command or just a social convenience? What can stop love growing cold? Or is Solzhenitsyn's sad observation always true?

> Every plant, every tree suffers the same fate – it hardens and grows a bark. Just as inevitably, a kind of bark grows and thickens on every love, and every marriage begins to petrify. It seems to be a natural law that as the years go by the urgency and desire of love must weaken.[6]

The biblical insistence on marriage as the proper context for sexual relationships is well known. Within marriage, sex binds together the relationship and holds the shared details of home-building in an ever-deepening union. It has no depth or significance by itself; those who see sex as meaningful apart from marriage, or merely as a means of procreation, have no support from Scripture. Sex creates a bond; but it is an insecure one unless the couple are prepared to share the *whole* of their lives with each other.

Dietrich Bonhoeffer, the German theologian, once said in a wedding sermon, 'It is not your love that sustains marriage, but from now on, the marriage that sustains your love.'[7] How un-romantic! But he has a point. Part of the nature of love is that lovers want to bind themselves to each other; a lack of commitment betrays a superficial love, however intense the feelings of passion may be. The structure of marriage provides the stability and security which is necessary if sinful human beings are not going to create social chaos and personal misery for themselves and their offspring every time love's feelings wane. And wane they will; Solzhenitsyn is right in so far as no couple can expect to live permanently on the crest of the wave of romance or sexual gratification. Physical tiredness, preoccupation with work or family affairs, and unexpected disagreements can all send the wave crashing against the rocks of indifference or even despair. But love which is genuinely concerned for the other as much – or more than – itself will ride out the storm and emerge from it all the stronger. In contrast to Solzhenitsyn's observation, C. S. Lewis testifies through his grief at the death of his wife that true unity and harmony can grow and last:

'One flesh, or, if you prefer, one ship. The starboard engine has gone. I, the port engine, must chug along somehow till we make harbour.'[8]

Sometimes, of course, things do turn sour. Human marriages do not always live up to their promise; sometimes they are built in a sandy base of mixed motives instead of the rock of love and trust, and slowly they topple as the storms beat upon them. God looks for faithfulness in all human relationships, just as he is faithful to the church which in Scripture is sometimes called 'the bride of Christ'. But even that bride can be faithless; even despite the love of her Head she can fail to live up to her promise. Failure of that sort grieves the Bridegroom and dishonours his name, just like the failure of human marriage, for whatever reason. The church is duty bound to maintain her public witness to the indissolubility of marriage, and to sanction divorce only in exceptional circumstances. But the gospel, paradoxically perhaps, is a gospel of new beginnings; failure is always a place where tragedy can lead out to triumph.

'The opportunity for putting all this into practice would be a fine thing!' I hear a single reader say. Because we live in a society where by far the majority of the over-twenty-five age group are married, married people tend to be insensitive to the feelings of the single person. Paul had some rather quaint things to say to the widows, bachelors and single women of his day: 'It is well for them to remain single as I do' (1 Corinthians 7:8). He seems to be making two points; first, he is giving us a much-needed reminder that sex and marriage are not the be-all and end-all of life. Secondly, he is suggesting that the single Christian can give a lot more time and energy to the service of Christ than can a married person who must give a great deal to their home life.

He must have known the intense loneliness of not having a special person to love and care for. I happen to believe that Paul was a widower rather than a bachelor;* if he was, it was probably even harder for him. He must have known the urgent drives of physical desire, too – and the liberating power of God's Spirit enabling him to lead a fulfilled and satisfying life without (further) sexual activity. How many married folk, let alone single ones, come to the end of their life and say with confidence and satisfaction, 'I have fought the good fight, I have finished the race, I have kept the faith' (2 Timothy 4:7)? So he should have known what he was talking about when he spoke of *both* married and single estates being 'gifts' of God (1 Corinthians 7:7) – gifts of the same order as the gifts of apostleship, evangelism, teaching, tongues and so on, because he uses the same word, *charisma*, for them all.

Our sexuality is an aspect of our humanity which is to be

* My evidence is rather slim: Jewish leaders like Paul were always married; in the verse quoted above 'remain' could refer to the state of being either widowed or single; and he does betray deep insights into marriage which bear the marks of experience.

brought within the purposes of a loving Creator, and which has an importance extending far beyond our personal life and circumstances.

> The political and social outlook of a historical group is more intimately conditioned by the sexual tone and attitude of its members than is usually assumed. The man who disavows responsibility in sexual matters will almost inevitably display irresponsibility in other areas of his life too. An . . . unprincipled concept of sex leads, perforce, to a disintegration of the social and political structure.[9]

It is to that social structure that we must now turn.

Follow-up

1. Look up these references which use marriage as a picture of God's relationship to his people. How should this affect our attitude to marriage (both before it and in it)? Hosea 2; Ephesians 5:21–33.
2. Notice how sexual union is jealously guarded and modesty strongly encouraged in Scripture. Consider how we can maintain a genuine respect for it and keep our sexuality in perspective in modern society. Leviticus 18:6–18; Deuteronomy 22:13–30; Matthew 19:3–12; 1 Corinthians 6:12—7:7; *cf.* Psalm 119:9; Matthew 5:27f.; Philippians 4:8.
3. What can we learn about the roles of men and women from the following references? How should we go about applying them? Judges 4:4f.; Proverbs 27:15; 31:10–31; Matthew 27:55f.; Acts 9:36–39; 1 Corinthians 7:17–24, 32–35; 1 Timothy 2:8–15.

References

[1] Jackie Stewart, *The Observer*, 21 December 1975.

[2] Shakespeare, *Romeo and Juliet*, I, i.

[3] Alexander Solzhenitsyn, *Cancer ward* (The Bodley Head, 1968), p. 183.

[4] David Gascoyne, 'An elegy', *Collected poems* (Oxford University Press, 1965).

[5] John Updike, *Couples* (Penguin, 1970), p. 295.

[6] Alexander Solzhenitsyn, *August 1914* (The Bodley Head, 1972), p. 131.

[7] Dietrich Bonhoeffer, quoted by Larry Christenson, *The Christian family* (Fountain Trust, 1971), p. 28.

[8] C. S. Lewis, *A grief observed* (Faber, 1966).

[9] Otto Piper, *The biblical view of sex and marriage* (Nisbet, 1960), p. 50.

'Human unity is not to be confounded with this modern industrial monotony and herding, which is rather a congestion than a communion.'
(G. K. Chesterton)

''Tis strange with how little notice, good, bad or indifferent, a man can live or die in London. He awakens no sympathy in the breast of any single person; his existence is a matter of interest to no-one save himself; and he cannot be said to be forgotten when he dies; for no-one remembered him when he was alive.'
(Charles Dickens)

5

Man in a mass

'It's everyone for himself these days!' said one harassed ticket collector to another as I and a hundred other hurrying commuters surged through the barrier one morning. For all we cared they might just as well have been a pair of automatic gates; in the rush for possessions, position and power we forget people. But people, of course, do not like to be forgotten; we want to feel that we are a meaningful and integral part of society.

Coming out of the station one night I noticed that someone had written on the wall, 'I was here.' A little further along the same hand had scrawled, 'and here.' The only way many people can hope to make a mark on the world is to do it literally. And when that happens, it says to us, as the writing on the wall said to king Belshazzar: 'You have been weighed in the balances and found wanting' (Daniel 5:27). We have created for ourselves a system in which the struggle for survival is no longer (in the West) a matter of fending off predatory beasts and finding enough food, but of maintaining our personal identity in an impersonal mass.

But as we have set about that task – and people have been especially concerned about the rights and needs of the individual ever since the industrial revolution threatened those rights and needs – we have sometimes lost sight of another important truth: that human individuality finds its fulfillment only in the company of others. An excessive individualism has permeated into the church as well, so that while the importance of personal reconciliation with God has been stressed, the equally important matters of the corporate life of the church have been neglected. The hippy movement and its associated communes in the 1960s heralded a return to a more healthy and biblical conception of man in society, but old traditions die hard and the change of emphasis from personal to corporate is not easy to make.

Yet the idea of 'corporate solidarity', which we met in chapters 1 and 2, is actually a common feature of modern society. The joint stock company is legally endowed with little less than a corporate personality: it can own property, buy and sell, employ people and make decisions. But 'it' is only a group of people. So, too, is a trade union or a political party or a football team. They each have a corporate identity which is more than the sum of the people who comprise it, and whose aim (but one which is not always achieved) is to work together smoothly *as one person*. Within these entities, the individual is ideally not usually swallowed up but given the opportunity to make his or her own contribution (although in practice this is not always the case).

But the ideal expresses something of the biblical concept of society: a group of people which is not an agglomeration but an association. I once watched one of Jacques Cousteau's films in which he had spotted from the air a large dark patch in the ocean. It was not an oil slick or a shadow, not a shallow or a wreck. When he sent his divers down, they discovered that the patch was a huge shoal of fish. Darting in and out, round and about, the individual fish were doing different things and moving in different directions, but the shoal itself was constant in shape, direction and speed of movement. In Scripture, human society is intended to be a corporate structure within which the individual finds his identity and is held personally responsible for what he does.

For that reason we find God portrayed as dealing with

groups – cities and even nations – as if they were one person. It is Israel as a whole that is punished for Achan's sin (Joshua 7). When Ezra the scribe discovered individuals who had broken God's law, he prayed that the nation might be forgiven for '*our* guilt' (Ezra 9:6); all are implicated in the misdeeds of the few. On the other hand a nation which honours God can be blessed by him (Psalm 33:12), although there is never any indication that every individual within it must be perfect first; the many people are implicated in the righteous decisions of the few leaders.

For that solidarity to work properly, it requires an ordered structure of law, a boundary fence showing fallen human beings what are the distinctions between social and anti-social conduct. And the moral law (summarized in the ten command-ments) recognizes that personal sin can in fact be as anti-social as public sin: covetousness, for instance, breeds envy, which breeds suspicion, which harms relationships. The law provides for leadership and authority to protect the weak and to punish the wayward. But it does not prevent bad men from abusing their power, and although Paul told the Roman Christians that 'rulers are not a terror to good conduct, but to bad' (Romans 13:3), the forces which ultimately led to Nero using the Christians as lion food were already at work. The principle, however, is sound, even if the practice is suspect; anarchy never works, even if democracy sometimes fails.

The law also has another weakness: it cannot force you and me to support one another even if it can stop us abusing one another. And so there is another biblical principle undergirding the concept of society: that of mutual care and love. The com-mand to 'love your neighbour as yourself' was given centuries before Jesus' parable of the good Samaritan (Leviticus 19:18; Luke 10:29–37). The slave was to be offered his freedom periodically, and the poor were to be allowed to glean food from the fields. 'Two are better than one,' says the author of

Ecclesiastes, ' . . . for if they fall, one will lift up his fellow' (4:9f.). Unfortunately the person who remembers that principle is usually the one left lying on his back. Cain's outburst, 'Am I my brother's keeper?' (Genesis 4:9) is more natural to sinful man than obedience to Paul's injunction to 'Count others better than yourselves' (Philippians 3:3). But it is in close family relationships that society finds its nucleus and its prototype.

The core of kids and the corps of kin

Every tribe and nation has some kind of family structure, but not all those structures are identical. In some communities polygamy is practised and in others monogamy is preserved. And in some communes there is a foreshadowing of Huxley's *Brave new world*: children are reared by professional parents unrelated to them.

To the Jews of the Bible, the close-knit nuclear family (mum, dad and the kids) provided the basic unit of society. The family lived and worked together; fortune and failure alike were shared together. It provided the structure within which the child found its security and learned the laws of God and of life. Discipline was strict but seen as a mark of love. 'He who spares the rod hates his son' said the sage (Proverbs 13:24), and the apostle does not demur: 'Children, obey your parents in the Lord, for this is right . . . Fathers, do not provoke your children to anger, but bring them up in the discipline and instruction of the Lord' (Ephesians 6:1, 4).

Most of all, the family was a window on the world. Aunts and uncles, grandparents and hired labourers (where the family were employers) would live and work in close proximity. This 'household', as it was known,* was a miniature society con-

* The modern idea of the 'extended family' is not exactly parallel; in the

taining a wide variety of temperaments and opinions and a broad spectrum of ages and roles. The sense of belonging together was inherent in the system – and has held the Israeli nation together for centuries despite successive dispersions across Europe and Asia.

Within our own society, close family ties have been loosened only since the industrial revolution, and they have lingered longest not in the affluent suburbs but among the socially under-privileged. Now, the soaring cost of housing has scattered young marrieds far and wide, while towering blocks of flats are destroying older, closer communities. Teenagers are encouraged to move away from the influence of the wider family to be herded together in the artificial communities of higher education where insecurity and stress are the price of a doubtful freedom. The culture gap between youth and age has widened so much that there are in effect two different *races* co-existing in uncertainty and tension. The television age has brought the world to our living-rooms and provided a substitute for human communication within households; little wonder that an emotional distance combines with geographical distance to separate members of families still further.

Now that she was too anginal and arthritic to live alone, he had stuck his mother into a Riversdale nursing home, instead of inviting her into his own spacious rooms, site of his dreary, sterile privacy. His father, in his position, would have become his mother's nurse. His grandfather would have become her slave. Six thousand years of clan loyalty were overturned in Bech.[1]

Novelist John Updike utters a prophet's lament. The weakening of family bonds had not only been one among several causes of the increasing impersonality of western

Jewish 'household' the nuclear families retained a considerable measure of independence and identity.

77

civilization. It has been a sin against humanity, eating away the very roots of human society planted by the Creator himself. For the biblical testimony concerning the family is that it is much more than a cultural convenience; it is part of the pattern of human life ordained by God, and in which he shared in the person of Jesus Christ.

Of course, there were black sheep even in New Testament times. The prodigal son (Luke 15:11ff.) was a figure who almost certainly had his counterparts in reality: for him fun took precedence over family solidarity. And the Pharisees made nonsense of the commandment to honour one's parents by allowing a religious gift to be a substitute for a personal obligation (Matthew 15:1–6). In the Old Testament the story of Joseph's rejection by his brothers is well known (Genesis 37), and the tragic family feud in which Absalom rose in futile rebellion against his father, king David, stands as a memorial to adolescent-like folly (2 Samuel 13–19). The family is society in microcosm; at times welcoming and secure, at times a restless, turbulent environment that we would rather be without.

A world of difference

Along the Jersey coast near St Helier there is a finger of rock poking out into the sea. At the end of this tiny peninsular stands a ruined stone hut where a hermit once lived. I have no idea why he cut himself off from the townsfolk. Perhaps he was psychologically sick. Or perhaps it was his way of protesting against the impersonal forces of society which threatened to smother his personal identity.

In his poem 'Prayer before birth' Louis MacNeice pleads:

O fill me
With strength against those who would freeze my
humanity, would dragoon me into a lethal automaton,
would make me a cog in a machine, a thing with
one face, a thing . . . [2]

As time goes on, it becomes increasingly difficult for you and me to consider ourselves important and indispensable parts of society, and to feel that the world will benefit a little from our contribution to it. We are caught up in a technological system that appears to have a mind of its own and which imposes its insatiable desire for expansion and innovation even upon those who are ostensibly in control of it. Man is mastered by the machine; he has become a sociological statistic memorized by a faceless computer and manipulated by a feelingless bureaucracy, while opportunities for creative work and community action become increasingly limited. The temptation to opt out completely is strong, but that does not solve the problem; indeed, as Robin Knox-Johnson discovered through his single-handed, non-stop voyage around the world:

> It is really no more possible to 'drop out' from a modern society to make the sort of voyage I planned than it is to drop-out in 'protest'; we depend on the continued support of others even to try.[3]

But in the face of an evil and impersonal society, many have tried to opt out, among them Christians. A string of esoteric communes of varying degrees of orthodoxy and heterodoxy threads its way through church history from the first century to the twentieth. Christians have always lived in an uneasy tension with the world. 'Do not love the world or the things in the world,' wrote the saintly John. 'If any one loves the world, love for the Father is not in him' (1 John 2:15). Even the practical and rather earthy James concurs: 'Whoever wishes to be a friend of the world makes himself an enemy of God' (4:4). According to Jesus it is the 'cares of the world' which threaten to choke the word of God (Matthew 13:22) and to gain one's life is of far greater value than to gain the world (Matthew 16:26).

Yet the New Testament also teaches that 'the meek . . . shall inherit the earth' (Matthew 5:5) and that God loved the world so much that he sent his Son into it (John 3:16). So it is not, as some of the more ascetic thinkers have believed, entirely evil and beyond the pale. In fact, the Hebrews thought of the world as a part of the creation of God which was originally 'very good' (Genesis 1:31). In New Testament times that faith had not been destroyed; in describing the majesty of Jesus, the letter to the Hebrews adds 'through whom also he created the world' which he continues to uphold 'by his word of power' (1:2f.). So is the world good or bad?

The biblical answer is, 'Neither;' although, in a sense, it is 'Both.' And believe it or not, I am not playing with words! The physical earth was created as something good; but human society is fallen, like the people who make it up. (Incidentally, Scripture teaches that the physical earth is corrupted by the fall; it is rather like a pot plant which was broken when the child carrying it stumbled and dropped it.) Whenever the New Testament uses the word 'world', it usually means *the world of men and affairs organized without reference (or in opposition) to God.*

Jesus himself made this clear in the prayer he uttered shortly before his betrayal. There, he spoke of his disciples as being 'not of the world, even as I am not of the world' (John 17:16). Jesus' 'home', the place to which he belonged, was not the world of men and affairs organized without reference to God; he belonged to a realm which centred on God. And so with you and me; when we become Christians we are born into a new way of life with God at its centre; our attitudes and our ambitions, our responses and our requirements, are no longer governed by 'worldly' criteria, but (slowly and imperfectly) by God's standards.

But Jesus is also at pains to point out that both he and his disciples none the less have their feet planted firmly on the ground. There is no room here for that brand of saintliness which is more akin to insensitive absent-mindedness. 'I do not pray that thou shouldest take them out of the world' – he knew the temptation of the religiously minded to shut themselves away in a monastery or a monochrome and exclusive church fellowship – 'but that thou shouldst keep them from the evil one' (John 17:15). He knew the pressures there would be from a world which preferred to shut God out of its affairs; those pressures were about to force nails through his hands and feet. But the workaday world in which he had hammered his thumbs and sawn his knuckles in the carpenter's shop was not to be despised simply because it turned his craft into a hideous cruelty. 'As thou didst send me into the world, so I have sent them into the world' (John 17:18). Born into a new realm with God at its centre, Christians are sent out into the old world which excludes God, to prove to that world that God cannot be excluded.

Paul makes the point even more clearly. His passion for the purity of the church and the holiness of the individual Christian had been misunderstood by the Corinthians. 'I wrote to you in my letter', he explained, 'not to associate with immoral men; not at all meaning the immoral of this world, or the greedy and robbers, or idolaters, since then you would need to go out of the world. But rather I wrote to you not to associate with any one who bears the name of brother if he is guilty of immorality or greed, or is an idolater, reviler, drunkard, or robber' (1 Corinthians 5:9ff.). Publicly to associate with such a person would appear to condone their behaviour as compatible with Christian faith. But in Corinth, where anything went in terms of behaviour, the distinctiveness of the gospel needed to be maintained clearly in that way.

'You are the salt of the earth,' Jesus told his disciples (Matthew 5:13). Salt can do its work of flavouring and preserving and purifying only if it has contact with the perishable article. 'You are the light of the world,' he went on (verse 16). A light can

6   81

show up the dirt and help people to find their way only if it is exposed on a stand rather than hidden under a tub.

But the 'you' here, as so often in Jesus' teaching, is plural, not singular. It is Christians as a group who are to be immersed within the society God himself entered; but there may be situations in which the individual is wise not to get involved. 'Lead us not into temptation' is a prayer that cannot be answered if we deliberately expose ourselves to those very situations in which we are likely to capitulate to the pressures of a morality and life-style that have nothing in common with Christianity. We need to be acutely aware of our own strengths and weaknesses, our motives and desires. But we also need to be aware of the unseen kingdom which is, like a tree, growing slowly, and at times imperceptibly, all around us,

King and country

'Are *you* the King of the Jews?' asked Pilate, gruffly. Only a week before, Jesus had ridden into Jerusalem and received a king's welcome; banner-waving crowds had flocked to see him and cheer him. 'Hosanna!' they cried. 'Blessed is he who comes in the name of the Lord, even the King of Israel!' (John 12:13). For three years the burden of Jesus' teaching had been what he had announced at the beginning: 'The time is fulfilled, and the kingdom of God is at hand; repent, and believe in the gospel' (Mark 1:15). And after the resurrection, in the first flush of incredulous excitement, the disciples gathered round their once-dead leader and asked, 'Lord, will you at this time restore the kingdom to Israel?' (Acts 1:6).

'*Are* you the King of the Jews?'

'My kingship is not of this world,' replied Jesus, gently. 'If my kingship were of this world, my servants would fight, that I might not be handed over to the Jews; but my kingship is not from the world' (John 18:33, 36).

'So you *are* a king?' Pilate was no fool; he dimly understood that Jesus was claiming a kingship of a kind which posed no threat to Caesar. 'He went out to the Jews again, and told them, "I find no crime in him" ' (verse 38).

'*My kingship is not of this world.*' Nothing to do with power-seeking or vote-chasing; not a matter of arms races and budget speeches. A king without a defined national territory; a kingdom without a common language or culture. Yet also a king to whom every other king must ultimately pay homage; and also a kingdom which one day shall cover the world. That much at least is clear from Scripture; God is king of the earth and will one day compel those who disregard his rule to acknowledge it.

Jesus confidently announced that the kingdom was not only future but also present. 'The kingdom of God is in the midst of you,' he told the Pharisees who asked him when it was coming (Luke 17:21). But what constitutes this kingdom? Augustine said that it was the world-wide church, and the Roman Catholics teach that today. That is not an unreasonable suggestion. One of the parables of the kingdom – that of the wheat and the weeds growing together in a field (Matthew 13:24f.) – is sometimes said to be a close parallel to the nature of the church with its mixture of the genuine and the spurious disciples.

The reformers, on the other hand, taught that the kingdom was a spiritual one, the totality of true believers but not any particular church organization. And Jesus made clear that the kingdom is a spiritual matter; it can be entered only by those who are 'poor in spirit' (Matthew 5:3) – those who recognize their poverty before God – and 'flesh and blood cannot inherit' it (1 Corinthians 15:50). But the problem with that is that it does not do justice to the implication that the kingdom is a community which is somehow recognizable. It is a wedding party (Matthew 22:2), characterized not by drunkenness or boring speeches but by 'righteousness and peace and joy in the

83

Holy Spirit' (Romans 14:17). And that has led some people to assume that the kingdom is a heaven after death, and others to assert that it is the reign of justice within communities on earth.

Now what is clear is that 'the kingdom of God' (or of 'heaven' as it is sometimes described) is not a realm but a rule; it is the fact of God's kingly rule. And its establishment is seen in Scripture to be more of the activity of God than of men; it is 'a kingdom prepared for you from the foundation of the world' (Matthew 25:34). In other words, its present manifestation is in the establishment of God's standards and rules within the world, as men and women, you and I, come under the claims of the Christian gospel and obey them. So it starts with the individual, is seen within a group of caring, righteous Christians, and spreads to the world around as others are influenced by the 'leavening' effect of Christians on society. That is how the kingdom, for the time being, receives its mixture of adherents; not all who are influenced by the 'leaven' actually acknowledge the king himself.

But it does mean that anyone can – and should – throw in their lot with those who are seeking to achieve a more just, peaceful and wholesome society, by just, peaceful and wholesome methods, for that is a part of the work that God is doing within the world. He will finally achieve that goal, and by his own methods, too; in the meantime we are under obligation to him to see that his rule is recognized and respected. And it is in the church where that obligation should be taken most seriously.

Rotting pews and real people

I once went to a mid-week meeting for young people which was known affectionately, but not officially, as 'The Lonely Hearts Club'. It wasn't difficult to see why. As I looked around at the hundred faces in the hall, loneliness was written across them all. Accountants and students, actresses and solicitors, articled clerks and secretaries, all alone in London. Every Wednesday night they could escape from the cold attic bed-sits with greasy gas rings and empty bread bins; they could emerge from the shared second-floor flats and leave behind them the constant plit-plat of tights dripping into the cracked enamel baths; they could enter a warm crowded hall and relax, meet people, make friends, feel welcome, forget work.

They were the lucky ones; they had somewhere to go, somewhere to belong. Then I remembered the thousands of others that I had passed on my way to the meeting, drifting around discos and dives, conned into believing that bright-coloured lights equal bright-coloured living. To say nothing of the older folks, equally lonely; the bachelors and spinsters out on the hunt for a spouse, or hunched resignedly in an easy chair watching the world go by on the television screen.

'Religion that is pure and undefiled before God and the Father is this: to visit orphans and widows in their affliction, and to keep oneself unstained from the world' (James 1:27). The orphan and widow were singled out by the apostle because in the ancient world they had no-one to care for them; they became the special concern of the early church. But I wonder what happens to the modern 'orphans', the single youths, or the modern 'widows', the middle-aged spinsters, who belong to no-one, and have none to care for them?

The church cared for the lonely and the needy in New Testament times. Despite its blemishes, it was a caring community. Possessiveness had given way to sharing and giving; isolation broke out into hospitality. Racial barriers collapsed, and a bond of joy and love united rich and poor, slave and free, young and old, married and single, man and woman. They saw themselves as 'a chosen race, a royal priesthood, a holy nation, God's own people' (1 Peter 2:9). This was a society, a kingdom, into which every true Christian was born and to which he belonged by right. Here was a corporate solidarity which respected the individual's personality; all were 'one body in Christ', but at the same time 'individually members one of another' (Romans 12:5). Here, in effect, was – and is – the nucleus of the new kingdom which God is building.

But, then as now, the local churches had their problems. The Corinthians, for instance, had learned a lot about giving, but they had more to learn about graciousness. The most common biblical picture of the church is that of a body; every part has an important function to play, however insignificant it may seem. But, like a body, the Christian church goes through sickness as well as health; it has blemishes on its skin and sometimes cancers grow on its bones. Sometimes it is weak and stumbling, like a toddler learning to walk. It is in its infancy still, despite the fact that 'it' has existed for two thousand years. 'It' has existed, but its constituent parts are for ever young. And, for that reason, full of potential.

> There is no life that is not in community,
> And no community not lived in praise of God.[4]

And with those words of T. S. Eliot, we must turn away from society with its centuries of history and focus our attention once more on ourselves, who are but a short-lived part of it.

Follow-up

1. What can you learn from these passages about the biblical concept of group solidarity? To what extent should it be applied to groups of non-related people? Genesis 36:6; Proverbs 14:34; Jeremiah 18:7-10; Romans 12:4-8.

2. What does the New Testament teach about the nature of the 'world' of men and affairs organized without reference to God? Matthew 18:7; Luke 12:30; John 1:10; 14:16f.; 16:33; 17:25;

1 Corinthians 2:12; Colossians 2:20.

3. Jesus told many parables about the kingdom of God. What truths about it do they teach? Matthew 13:18–52; 18:23–35; 20:1–16; 22:1–14; 25:1–30.

References

[1] John Updike, *Bech: a book* (Andre Deutsch, 1965), p. 118.
[2] Louis MacNeice, 'Prayer before birth', *Collected poems*, ed. E. R. Dodds (Faber, 1966), p. 193.
[3] Robin Knox-Johnson, *A world of my own* (Cassell, 1969), p. 32.
[4] T. S. Eliot, 'Choruses from "The Rock"', *Selected poems* (Faber, 1961), p. 114.

'I honestly do not think I am unfair to the whole trend of the time if I say that it is intellectually irritated; and therefore without that sort of rich repose in the mind which I mean when I say that a man when he is alone can be happy because he is alive.'
(G. K. Chesterton)

'If there were no such thing as death the whole human race could be happy.'
(Kingsley Amis)

6

Dust and destiny

One of the great art classics of all time is Michelangelo's painting on the ceiling of the Sistine Chapel in Rome. Biblical and legendary characters are portrayed in a vigorous style, linked together in a complex pattern of symbolism with at times deep spiritual insight.

But one fact above all strikes the visitor when he first looks inside the door; he cannot see the whole ceiling by standing in the doorway. In fact, he cannot see it all by standing anywhere. Michelangelo painted the ceiling so that it had to be viewed from several different positions; the visitor has to keep moving round the chapel if he is to make any sense of the figures and gain an over-all understanding of the whole work.

And that is true also of the biblical 'painting' of human nature. The whole cannot be understood from one vantage point only. In describing man, the biblical writers, as it were, move around him, seeing him now from one angle, now from another. He is a being of such complex unity that a view from a single angle leads only to a distorted understanding of the whole. Analytical lists of the contents, and close-up views of tiny sections, do not present a true impression of the totality of man.

Modern man is obsessed by analysis and subdivision. Everything must be catalogued; everything must be reduced to its basic components. But analysis is restricting as well as revealing; a single tree interests a botanist but a wood intrigues a poet. Subdivision can be destructive as well as definitive; the atomic mushroom hangs in the sky as a memorial to the division of the basic unit of matter – nature's protest at being stripped naked and skinned, at having her vitals removed and preserved in insulated cans of instability.

So, too, with human nature. Analyse it *ad infinitum* and you are left not with a person but with a patchwork of electrical impulses and electrifying complexes. Subdivide it into components and the product will be as unstable as a bomb. When one aspect of the personality is exalted above, or debased beneath, the rest, the bomb is activated. When that one aspect is pursued or persecuted the bomb is exploded and the blast throws someone still further from the goal of mature humanity.

The Christian church has not been blameless in the affair. At times we have preached to souls but neglected stomachs; we have planted new churches but pulled down natural cultures. One generation of Christians has detested emotion in worship, only to be replaced by one that is indifferent to reason in witness. Whatever the over- or under- emphasis, the result is always the same: a perverted gospel is proclaimed and a poverty-stricken Christianity is practised.

Yet the biblical description of man gives no room for this attitude. Although the Bible uses words like 'body', 'flesh', 'mind', 'heart', 'soul' and 'spirit', it does not use them as exactly as we often do. They are not usually definitions of the various parts of the human personality; they are largely *descriptions of the vantage point of the writer*. They are imprecise terms which frequently overlap. Quite often, they can be replaced by 'you' or 'I', with the loss of depth of insight, but not of strict accuracy. This is nowhere more clearly seen than in the case of 'body' and 'soul'.

The dust of life

'A pair of pincers set over a bellows and a stewpan, and the whole thing fixed upon stilts.'[1] That was how Samuel Butler in the eighteenth century rather cynically described the human body. More usually, man has been fascinated and amazed by his complex physique; although versions of the Bible disagree over whether or not the psalmist actually wrote 'I am fearfully and wonderfully made' (Psalm 139:14, AV), the sentiment has been felt and expressed by many.

The body is certainly a phenomenal piece of equipment. Its light but tough structure of 206 bones, accounting for only one-fifth of the body's weight, is mobilized into smooth and often intricate action by over 600 muscles. Lungs containing over 300 million tiny air sacs, the membranes of which, if spread out, would cover 56 square metres, provide oxygen for the bloodstream. Some 97,000 *kilometres* of tubing carry blood to every extremity; $6\frac{1}{2}$ litres of life-sustaining fluid are pumped round the body a thousand times a day. Fuel from a variety of foods is broken down by home-made secretions in 6 metres of flexible intestine. A built-in waste-disposal system and a resident corps of maintenance engineers work non-stop to keep the body fit and healthy. Intricate micro-mechanisms provide sight and sound, smell, touch and taste, while the brain (packing into its $1\frac{1}{2}$ kg, 15 cm diameter mass, the work-power of a computer the size of a skyscraper) turns these instincts into senses. The whole is remarkably durable and frequently long-lived, emerges from the womb complete, and is covered in a waterproof, easy-to-clean protective skin less than half a centimetre at its thickest.

Yet despite the complex inter-dependence of all its delicately-balanced organs, 95% of the body's weight is accounted for by only six of the most common elements (oxygen, hydrogen, nitrogen, carbon, calcium and phosphorous) and over 60%

of it is actually fluid. While we are probably used to the body being described as a collection of chemicals, it may come as something of a surprise to discover that the Bible takes a similar view. We are formed of 'dust from the ground' (Genesis 2:7; *cf.* 1 Corinthians 15:47) and eventually, 'the dust returns to the earth as it was' (Ecclesiastes 12:7).

The Bible writers have a robust and realistic view of the body, and over eighty parts of the anatomy are named in the Old Testament alone. The physical functions which some consider too indelicate to mention are, as every schoolboy discovers to his delight as he flips through its pages during an exceptionally boring Scripture lesson, treated without comment as a normal fact of life. To the Hebrew, human life *was* physical life; it could be nothing else, which is why life after death receives such scanty treatment until the physical resurrection of Jesus. Above all, the body is viewed as a vital part of the creation which 'was very good' (Genesis 1:31).

This immediately sets the Bible over against a number of ancient and modern views. The Greek philosophers several centuries before Christ considered all physical matter to be inherently evil. Plato once wrote, 'If we are ever to know anything we must be freed from the body.'[2] These ideas filtered into the Christian church, and some sects known as the Gnostics denied the reality of Jesus' body; in their opinion a holy God could not defile himself with human flesh. Every generation has had its flagellating monks and fasting hermits who paradoxically expended volumes of energy trying to subdue the legitimate appetites as well as the excessive desires of the body. Today, the Christian Science sect denies the reality of the body; according to its teaching, matter does not exist. Some of the increasingly popular eastern cults fall somewhere between this and the Greek view.

The Bible does not for one moment deny that the human body is part of fallen human nature. When Paul tells us that the body is 'dead because of sin' (Romans 8:10) however, he goes on to remind us that the body is included in man's redemption by Jesus Christ (verse 23). When he refers to 'the sinful body' in Romans 6:6, the context makes it clear that Paul means 'the body through which sin is expressed'. That provides the key to the scriptural view of the body; it is not a part of human nature detached from the rest; it is man's physical expression of himself. In Scripture, 'body' means *man in God's image viewed as a finite, physical, and therefore mortal, being.*

Indeed, far from condemning the body, the Bible commends it as worthy of care and attention.* 'Your body is a temple of the Holy Spirit within you,' says Paul (1 Corinthians 6:19). The word 'temple' is the usual one for the sacred inner sanctuary, the Holy of holies, the place of God's presence, in the Jewish temple. 'So', he continues, 'glorify God in your body.' On another occasion he exhorted the Roman Christians to 'present your bodies as a living sacrifice, holy and acceptable to God, *which is your spiritual worship*' (Romans 12:1). 'Worship' is the normal word for a church service; yet it would be true to say that instead of treating our bodies with dignity, many of us sacrifice them to the god of gluttony and the idol of idle indulgence.

We in the affluent West stuff our bellies with disproportionate quantities of protein while the begging-bowls of two-thirds of our fellow humans remain empty. We clog our pores with cosmetics and coat our lungs with tar. We rot our teeth with excessive sugar and ruin our muscles by travelling vast distances without moving one of them. We spend millions removing the excess weight which is regarded by society as a fashionable disability rather than a physical disgrace. We spend millions more on proprietory pharmaceuticals which our

* It is well known that Paul uses the term 'flesh' very disparagingly. As we shall see in chapter 8, however, he does not use the word literally for the human body, but technically as a description of the whole man as a fallen being, alienated from God.

93

fastidiousness demands but which our organic functions do not require.

It is easy to be negative, but the Bible is always positive. It recognizes that much of our time will normally be spent on providing for the physical needs of ourselves and our families, but provision is not to become a preoccupation. 'Is not life more than food, and the body more than clothing?' asks Jesus (Matthew 6:25). To those of us who live in order to eat, rather than eat in order to live, comes the reminder that 'man does not live by bread alone, but . . . by everything that proceeds out of the mouth of the Lord' (Deuteronomy 8:3). But that does not give us a licence to neglect the needs of others. 'If a brother or sister is ill-clad or in lack of daily food,' says James, 'and one of you says to them, "Go in peace, be warmed and filled," without giving them the things needed for the body, what does it profit?' (James 2:15f.).

Medical pioneers like Joseph Lister, missionary pioneers like Hudson Taylor, modern relief agencies like TEAR Fund, have followed James' advice and Jesus' example. People are not merely machines requiring fuel and repairs. Nor are they abstract entities to be fished for and drawn into a net. Jesus fed as well as taught; he preached and also healed. He treated every individual as a complete person, which is precisely what the word 'soul' means in Scripture.

Living dust

For centuries philosophers and theologians have competed with one another to define the nature of the soul. The ordinary person has not been a disinterested spectator of the contest; he has been more in the position of a tennis ball in the finals at Wimbledon. It is *his* soul that is being knocked around the experts' court; his beliefs, his destiny, have been at stake.

The Greeks were the chief architects of the two-tier conception of man. Reality, they said, was pure, eternal and spiritual. The body was evil, mortal and material. Man, however, appeared to be a combination of these apparently mutually exclusive entities; although a physical being he had a psychical nature. So the philosophers taught that man possessed an intermediary soul, an emanation of spirit entombed in a body. Salvation involved the release of the soul from its phsyical prison.

The ordinary citizens of Athens did not, of course, think of it in such clinical terms; the belief was a religious creed long before it became a philosophical concept. The origin of the soul was depicted in one of the sagas for which the Greeks were famous. After Prometheus had fashioned the human body, it was said that Eros brought it to life and Athene gave it an immortal soul so that man could love and worship the gods.

The influence of Greek thought upon the church was such that official Christian teaching readily adopted the Greek view of body and soul.* One theologian, Origen, taught the pre-existence of the soul; souls that had sinned in a previous life were put on earth imprisoned in human bodies. The view was condemned as un-biblical by a church council in Constantinople in AD 543, and implicit in the decision was a rebuttal of all ideas of reincarnation.

One the greatest church controversies has been over the origin of the soul. The 'creationists' claimed that every human being was given a newly created soul by God; they disagreed over whether this was at conception or at birth. The 'traducianists' believed that soul and body alike were inherited from our parents and ultimately descended from Adam himself. This

* With hindsight we can perhaps see the inconsistency of this more clearly. In both Greek and Christian thought, man reflects the nature of God. The God of the Scriptures is a unity (even though a trinity); the Greek gods were many and constantly at war with each other. We have absorbed a concept of man which contradicts our view of God.

'apparently hopeless controversy' based on 'dubious' scriptural evidence[3] has continued to the present day and the creationist view is part of the Roman Catholic argument in the abortion debates.

Secular philosophers have argued over the very existence of the soul. René Descartes, the father of 'rationalist' philosophy, said in the eighteenth century that the soul (or mind) was man's inner nature, a separate entity with its own processes and powers. Nonsense, replied his fiercest critic, there are no inner processes comparable to physical processes; the whole idea is the fable of 'the ghost in the machine'.[4] Even psychologists have introduced a concept of soul into their discussions. Viktor Frankl defines it as 'the core or nucleus of the personality' and states that, 'The goal of psychotherapy is to heal the soul, to make it healthy; the aim of religion is . . . to save the soul'.[5] He is careful, however, to avoid defining what he means by 'save'.

So it almost seems that 'soul' can be what you or I care to make it. That many be convenient, but it is also confusing – especially as the Bible uses the word over 850 times.* Despite the fact that the Authorized Version has forty-two different renderings of the one Hebrew word, the meaning of 'soul' is comparatively clear and simple, it challenges our popular beliefs and begins to open up a whole new dimension to our understanding of human nature: the dimension of human destiny.

The biblical uses of 'soul' fall under three closely related headings. It can mean man seen as a *living* person, with the emphasis on 'living'. 'Soul' is someone's natural human life

* It should be noted that whilst the Old Testament was originally written in Hebrew and the New Testament in Greek, many words, including 'soul' (and 'heart' and 'spirit' which we shall consider later) have the same basic meaning in both. Old and New Testaments share the same thought-forms and world-view, although there are discernible developments of understanding as God's revelation unfolds through the historical period covered by the Bible.

(another word is used in the New Testament for the eternal life bestowed on the Christian by Jesus Christ). Thus at the creation of man we read: 'The Lord God formed man of dust from the ground, and breathed into his nostrils the breath of life; and man became a living being (literally, soul)' (Genesis 2:7). The word is quite often translated as 'life'; the psalmist is troubled by his enemies 'who seek after my life' (Psalm 35:4), whilst the exploits of Paul and Barnabas earn them the reputation of 'men who had risked their lives' (Acts 15:26).

Secondly 'soul' is a synonym for 'yourself' or 'myself'; it is man seen as a living *person*, with the emphasis on 'person'. Thus Isaiah's prophecy of the death of Jesus is translated 'he makes himself (literally, his soul) an offering for sin' (Isaiah 53:10); Jesus died physically; he sacrificed his whole person. On the day of Pentecost 'about three thousand souls' heard about the risen Jesus and believed in him (Acts 2:41); soul stands for 'people'. Paul reminds some of his converts that 'we were ready to share with you not only the gospel of God but also our own selves' (1 Thessalonians 2:8); Christian witness is not only a matter of saying the words but also of self-giving on behalf of the hearers.

The third use of 'soul' is concerned with personal experience; it is man seen as a *living-person*, as a whole being who is aware of himself and his surroundings. A glance at the pages of a concordance reveals a wide range of emotions and experiences attributed to the soul (and which are frequently attributed to both 'heart' and 'spirit' also): affection and love (1 Samuel 18:1; Song of Solomon 1:7); depression and vexation (Psalm 42:5; 2 Peter 2:8); joy and worship (Psalm 35:9; Luke 1:46). It is the soul, the living person, who can keep God's law (Psalm 119:167), seek pleasure or crave wickedness (Proverbs 13:4; 21:10). It is the soul, the whole man, who is kept sound, purified, and finally saved (Acts 14:22; 1 Peter 1:22; James 1:21).

Being designed in the image of God gives you and me an identity; being designated 'living souls' gives to our personalities a built-in integrity. The Bible treats us as whole persons, and tells us that God does likewise. That may not sound very novel, but it is certainly very noble; we do not always accord ourselves or others such dignity. Instead we magnify the strong points of our characters and the weak points of others', falsely assuming that they represent the true 'self'. Perhaps that is because, as fallen humans, we are content with our incompleteness. The searching eye of God, penetrating to every nook and cranny, seeing all because seeing the whole, is too uncomfortable to take seriously. But we cannot avoid his gaze for ever.

Life after dust

'Meet St Paul tonight – touch the buried wires.' So a workman wrote on the pavement near my office one evening when he left a half-finished electrical job at the traffic lights. We joke nervously about death, putting on a bold front in the face of an enemy we know we cannot defeat. 'What man can live and never see death?' (Psalm 89:48).

You and I live in a world of dying people and we grow familiar with the obituary notices in the press and the pictures of bodies lying in the streets. Yet when death strikes a person close to us, numbed with shock we gaze in disbelief at something which seems so unreal. The mourning friend curses because the suicide might have been avoided 'if only I'd phoned'. The bereaved husband or wife re-lives the rows and failures, hoping vainly for the opportunity to say 'sorry'. Their hot streaming eyes look longingly into the coffin but meet only a cold sightless stare in reply. The finality and futility of death makes frustration all the more deep. 'You are dust, and to dust you shall return' (Genesis 3:19).

She came out of the crematorium, and there from the twin towers above her head fumed the very last of Fred, a thin stream of grey smoke from the ovens. People passing up the flowery surburban road looked up and noted the smoke; it had been a busy day at the furnaces. Fred dropped in indistinguishable grey ash on the pink blossoms: he became part of the smoke nuisance over London, and Ida wept.[6]

Most of us react in the face of death like Graham Greene's Ida; and in their dying more people react like Jesus the Messiah than like Socrates the Stoic. Socrates, talking cheerfully, bade his friends farewell, calmly drank the hemlock, and died. Jesus in the garden of Gethsemane shrank in fear from his coming execution; he cried in the agony of pain and the awefulness of desolation as he hung limply on the cross. The former has been praised and the latter pitied; but it was Jesus who was the realist, not Socrates.

Death is always viewed in Scripture as ugly and hateful. Like the human sinfulness with which it is always linked, it is an intruder into God's universe. It is no use speculating how the transition from earthly to heavenly life would have occurred if man had not sinned. Man *has* sinned, and the death which is 'the wages of sin' (Romans 6:23) is mortality as well as exclusion from God's presence.* *And physical mortality is the end of human existence.* Nothing whatever survives death; that is the biblical testimony; that is the ugliness of death; that is the conclusion of the scriptural view of body and soul.

* See above, chapter 2, for a discussion of this latter sense of 'death', which is frequent in the New Testament. The example of Enoch, who 'was taken up so that he should not see death' (Hebrews 11:5) is the only one which hints at 'translation', although Elijah's 'chariots of fire' (2 Kings 2:11) could be another. C. S. Lewis's novel, *Out of the silent planet* (The Bodley Head, 1938), has a fascinating account of 'translation'. On the sinless planet Malacandra, 'death is not preceded by dread nor followed by corruption' (p. 180). Lewis takes us to the far borders of speculation; the Bible reserves its revelation until after the one event of which we can now all be certain.

It may take a few moments for the fact to sink in. It is a fact that human beings are rarely willing to accept: indeed, only humanists and Christians can accept it, the former because it is the logical outcome of their world-view and the latter because they believe that, none the less, God has provided an answer to the dilemma. Dr James Bedford did not accept it; that American psychologist left several thousand dollars in his will so that his body could be deep-frozen in the hope that techniques of resuscitation would be discovered.[7] The man in the street refuses to accept it; he obstinately asserts that 'there must be something beyond this world'. The more practical-minded mourners follow the Egyptian superstition that immortality is lost if the body perishes, and buy expensive embalming and concrete vaults from the undertaker. Even life insurance becomes a religion rather than a responsibility; a man lives on in his family: a surprising modern version of the ancient practice of ancestor worship. Perhaps that just goes to show that men and women are still aware that, as people in God's image, they are not made simply in order that they should die.

'Immortality' occurs only twice in the Bible.* It belongs to God alone (1 Timothy 6:16), yet our mortal human nature will 'put on immortality' (1 Corinthians 15:23, 54). The second reference opens up the incredible biblical answer to the death that stalks you and me. For, says Paul in that passage, death itself is to be done away with. No half-measures of an immortal soul clinging on to its life and bidding farewell to the rest; no eternal defeat for one part of God's creation, the physical realm. Instead, 'death is swallowed up in victory' (verse 54).

When death is removed, the creation is renewed and the body resurrected. Not the old, wrinkly body with its creaky joints and clumsy fingers, but a new kind of body to express the renewed personality. Life after death for the Christian means

* Another word which means 'incorruption' (a different thing) is translated 'immortality' in Romans 2:7 and 2 Timothy 1:10.

completion. The personality fragmented by the fall is drawn together in an unshakeable unity. The imperfections of our physical body will not be merely removed; they will be perfected in our resurrection body. The inadequacy of our understanding will not be merely corrected; it will become complete: 'Now I know in part; then I shall understand fully, even as I have been understood' (1 Corinthians 13:12). The unreliability of our emotions will not be merely steadied; we will learn to laugh and sing for joy for the very first time.

This is not the wishful thinking of the inadequate or incompetent fringe of society, as some would have us believe. The evidence for this hope can be examined, because in the resurrection of Jesus God has already demonstrated what he will one day do for all his followers. 'Just as we have borne the image of the man of dust, we shall also bear the image of the man of heaven... Thanks be to God, who gives us the victory through our Lord Jesus Christ' (1 Corinthians 15:49, 57).

But that lies in the future, as far as you and I as persons are concerned, and as far as this book is concerned. In the meantime, we must change our vantage point. The God of the Bible is a very searching counsellor: 'Thou art acquainted with all my ways' (Psalm 139:3). Having seen that people are undivided, mortal and physical beings, we must now try to penetrate that uniquely human phenomenon: the invisible 'heart' with its rich variety of feelings.

Follow-up

1. What practical examples and advice can be found in the Bible concerning care for the body? What *principles* lie behind the details and how can they be applied in your situation? Proverbs 15:16f.; 22:9; 24:33f.; Psalm 127:2; Daniel 1:8–16; Matthew 6:24–34; Luke 8:3; 10:38–42; 1 Timothy 4:1–5, 8; 5:23.

2. Look up the following verses and discuss the meaning of 'soul' in each case. (Some versions may not always use the word 'soul', although the RSV does use it in each verse cited. In many instances in Scripture, 'soul' is translated by 'I' or 'self' or 'life' and no indication is given in the English that the word in fact is 'soul'.) Genesis 34:3; 1 Samuel 1:15; Psalm 24:4; Isaiah 1:4; Ezekiel 18:4; Matthew 11:29; 26:38; Luke 2:35; 12:19f.; Acts 14:22; 1 Peter 4:19.

3. Read 1 Corinthians 15. How does Paul argue the case for the resurrection of the body? How does he describe that body? What is his attitude to the physical body?

References

[1] Quoted by Alan Nourse, *The body* (Time-Life International, 1969), p. 8. I am indebted to this book for most of the largely irrelevant but highly intriguing statistics which I have included in the paragraph following the one containing the quotation.

[2] Quoted by William Barclay, *Flesh and spirit* (SCM, 1962), p. 11.

[3] G. C. Berkouwer, *Man: the image of God* (IVP, 1973), p. 307.

[4] Gilbert Ryle, *The concept of mind* (Hutchinson, 1963), p. 27.

[5] Viktor E. Frankl, *The doctor and the soul* (Souvenir Press, 1969), p. 8; *cf.* p. xv.

[6] Graham Greene, *Brighton rock* (Heinemann and The Bodley Head, 1970), pp. 40f.

[7] Cited by Rattray-Taylor, *The biological timebomb* (Book Club Associates, 1968).

'I think that presence of mind is far more really poetical than absence of mind.'
(G. K. Chesterton)

'With an unquiet mind, neither exercise, nor diet, nor physick can be of much use.'
(Dr Samuel Johnson)

7
Heart-throbs and headaches

King Richard I of England earned himself the title 'The Lion-heart' through his cruel but heroic deeds during the third Crusade. John Bunyan called one of the cowardly rogues who hindered Pilgrim's progress 'Faint-heart'. Most of us probably know of a generous old uncle Bert who is 'large-hearted' in distributing presents to his nieces and nephews, and a kind, 'warm-hearted' aunt Molly, always smiling and hospitable. We do not need reminding of the selfish attitude of 'hard-hearted' Joe, and we feel sad when we remember 'broken-hearted' Jean, jilted by her boyfriend.

Popular thought has always linked human feelings with the heart, and the Bible is no exception. The symbolism is so universal that it is impossible to dismiss the one-thousand Old and New Testament references to 'heart' as primitive attempts to root non-material experiences to a part of the body. (Behaviourist psychology does, of course, attempt to do just that by tracing feelings to genes and glands.)

The Bible writers do not present us with a concise theory of psychology or an established code of psychiatric practice. They do show, however, a deep insight into the workings of the human psyche, and in their use of 'heart' to describe feelings, thoughts, the will and the subconscious levels of personality, stress the unity of the human being which we began to see in the previous chapter. In Scripture, 'heart' means 'the focus of the personal life';[1] *it views the whole man, created in God's image, from the angle of his inner consciousness.* And what could be more personal, and more incomprehensible, than our emotions?

Reasonable emotion

'Do you know what "le vice Anglais" – the English vice – really is?' asks Sebastian Cruttwell in Terence Rattigan's play *In praise of love.* 'Not flagellation, not pederasty – whatever the French believe it to be. It's our refusal to admit to our emotions. We think they demean us, I suppose.'[2]

The Italians weep publicly for joy or sorrow. The Americans greet one another with broad grins and hearty handshakes; the French and the Russians with a hug and a kiss. The British, famous for their 'stiff upper lip', rarely display their emotions.

Now national character is part of national culture. Neither the British nor the Latin temperament is intrinsically more godly than the other; God has created varieties of humans just as he has created varieties of hollyhocks. But God himself is not without feeling, although he is not moody and capricious like you and me. He can be grieved by human sinfulness (Genesis 6:6; Ephesians 4:30) and angered by open rebellion (Isaiah 5:25). He shows kindness and love to us (Titus 3:4). Jesus spoke of 'glory' in his Father's presence, which must include something amounting to enjoyment and satisfaction (John 17:24). For man in God's image, feelings are a legitimate part of experience.

The whole gamut of emotions is catalogued in the Psalms. 'Thou hast put . . . joy in my heart' (4:7). 'My heart is glad, and my soul rejoices' (16:9). 'Thou hast given him his heart's desire' (21:2). 'My heart shall not fear' (27:3). 'The Lord is near to the broken-hearted, and saves the crushed in spirit' (34:18). 'Their hearts were bowed down with hard labour' (107:12). 'His heart is steady, he will not be afraid' (112:8).

The Bible does not allow these emotions to displace the

intellect. In a word, they are rational. A thought is not rational because it is a thought; it is rational only when it is in accord with all the facts. I may consider myself to be the Shah of Persia, but my bank balance and my passport will not bear me out: I am being irrational. An emotion is rational when it is the appropriate human response to a given situation. It is appropriate to 'rejoice with those who rejoice (and) weep with those who weep' (Romans 12:15); it is inappropriate and irrational to laugh and joke in the presence of a weeping mourner. Perhaps more frequently we would use the word 'justified'; I am justified in being angry when you are late if you are just being lazy, but not if your train broke down and you had to wait for another.

There are numerous examples of rational and irrational emotions in the Bible. Take Elijah, for instance. Like many of us, he once found circumstances just too difficult to bear, and he fled into the desert and asked God to take away his life (1 Kings 18–19). His feelings were understandable; he was mentally exhausted after a long struggle with pagan priests, and physically tired and hungry after a hundred-mile dash to escape the murderous queen Jezebel. Elijah needed food and rest, and these he was given. And then he became irrational. Instead of reviewing the situation and seeking God's plan for the next phase of his work, he just ran further away, feeling sorry for himself and quite blind to the true facts. He thought he was an isolated believer; but he had been too busy to notice there were thousands of others. He thought God had failed; but he had forgotten the odds-against victories of the past.

Then there is Jesus, who wept when his friend Lazarus died. Grief is never an easy emotion to deal with, and only a shallow love feels no pain when someone close is suddenly taken away. The onlookers commented on Jesus' tears: 'See how he loved him!' (John 11:36). The cruel comfort, 'You'll soon get over it,' and the well-meaning jibe, 'He's better off this way,' find no precedent in Scripture; tears are right, tears are rational. What is not rational, for the Christian, is the feeling of hopelessness which aggravates grief. Paul writes in some detail about the state of the dead: 'We would not have you ignorant, brethren . . . that you may not grieve as others do who have no hope' (1 Thessalonians 4:13).

Turning to the other end of the emotional spectrum, there is no joylessness in Scripture; faith is not incompatible with fun. Christians have sometimes encountered a quite irrational feeling of guilt about ordinary relaxation and enjoyment. The psalmist tells us that God created 'wine to gladden the heart of man, (and) oil to make his face shine' (104:15), and Jesus seemed quite at home at the Jewish weddings and dinner parties he attended. On one occasion Paul and Silas appeared to be acting irrationally – even dementedly – when they sang hymns at midnight while locked in the far from comfortable prison at Philippi (Acts 16:25). On this and other similar occasions, it was their previous experience of, and deep faith in, a sovereign God which prompted their rejoicing. God had not changed nor had he deserted them, even though they were in danger; their emotions were fully in accord with the facts, and quite appropriate.

But while the Bible is in many ways a joyful book, it never countenances the pursuit of happiness as an end in itself. The author of Ecclesiastes declared this to be quite irrational, 'a striving after wind', when he had tried it out for himself (2:10f.). And while Paul says in one place that the killjoys 'who forbid marriage and enjoin abstinence from foods' have 'departed from the faith' (1 Timothy 4:1-3), he points out in another that one person's freedom can be someone else's bondage. ' "All things are lawful," but not all things build up. Let no one seek his own good, but the good of his neighbour' (1 Corinthians 10:23f.). Helpfulness to all is a more important criterion than the happiness of a few. Church history is full of instances where excess has led to schism; feeling and thought must walk hand in hand.

Emotional reason

Reason distinguishes man from the animals more clearly than any other attribute. Dogs may display loyalty and dolphins may devise their own games, but only people think abstractly and argue cogently.

Man has often been proud of his superior intelligence. Reason was deified by the Greeks and defended in the Renaissance; it was adored by nineteenth-century innovators and analysed by twentieth-century investigators. More recently, however, reason has become suspect; philosophers have argued that knowledge is illusory and scientists have discovered how little they understand. A rising generation has rejected the rationalism which created the atomic bomb; and their parents, confronted by the plethora of general-knowledge magazines, frequently decide that comparative ignorance is likely to lead to comparative bliss, even if not to considerable wealth.

Christians have varied considerably in their attitude to the intellect. The Inquisitors forced the Italian astronomer and physicist, Galileo, to renounce his belief that the earth revolved round the sun. Some Christians have subordinated the labour of thought to the instinctiveness of the spirit, and at least one sect has forbidden converted students to continue their 'unspiritual' secular studies. At the other extreme, theologians at times have been all too ready to adapt their beliefs to the most recent scholarly theory.

The Bible rates human rationality as highly as any other human faculty. 'It is the spirit in a man, the breath of the Almighty, that makes him understand' (Job 32:8); in other words, thought is a consequence of being made in God's image. We are to be like the Lord who 'is a God of knowledge'

(1 Samuel 2:3) and 'not like a horse or a mule, without under-standing, which must be curbed with bit and bridle' (Psalm 32:9).

True knowledge derives from God and is the mainspring of responsible human action: 'The fear of the Lord is the begin-ning of wisdom, and the knowledge of the Holy One is insight' (Proverbs 9:10). For this reason the man who 'says in his heart, "There is no God," ' is quite uncompromisingly called 'the fool' (Psalm 14:1); he has shut himself out from the source of full understanding. That is not to say that the only knowledge worth having concerns God; certainly the facts of the gospel of Jesus Christ are commended to human study as matters 'of first importance' (1 Corinthians 15:3), but we are not denied the liberty of exploring the fascinating and mystifying details of God's world over which we have been granted dominion.

The Hebrews always conceived of knowledge as something dynamic, a matter of commitment rather than mere assent. They had no time for impersonal and abstract rationalism, but they were none the less passionately concerned with the deep-est questions of life and death. Paul, for example, was a man of immense intellect who explored the mind-stretching depths of God's eternal purposes. He was neither unable nor unwilling to debate with the Athenian philosophers, but while they wanted to be entertained by ideas, he was enthusing about truth (Acts 17).

At least part of the reason for this was that Paul did not share the Stoic view that the mind was a distinct entity within a person, a toy or a tool granted to man by the gods to aid and abet the human cause. Although he used Greek words for rational processes, he retained the Hebrew concept which related thought to the other psychological activities of 'the heart'. In Genesis it is stated that 'every imagination of the thoughts of (man's) heart was only evil continually' (6:5). 'Jesus, knowing their thoughts, said, "Why do you think evil in your hearts?" ' (Matthew 9:4). Paul uses 'heart' for 'mind' when he writes of the 'darkened' minds of those who have rejected God (Romans 1:21).

This symbolic usage cannot be explained simply as physiological ignorance. Experience shows us that thought and feeling are closely intertwined. When you went shopping today your thoughts which chose packs and assessed prices were mixed up with feelings that fancied certain clothes and desired certain foods. As you think about these pages you are either feeling bored to tears or else you are (I hope!) growing in your awareness of what it means to be a human being. Unfortunately we frequently deprive ourselves of part of our humanness by prizing a memory for facts above the wisdom which applies those facts and the worship which appreciates them.

Most of us have, in the phrase of John Betjeman, 'tinned minds'. We preserve our pre-packed prejudices and air-tight attitudes in a syrup of sentiment. We live at such a pace that instinctive reactions and instant replies are constantly demanded of us. We do not have the time – and we easily lose the inclination – to think out matters slowly and deliberately. We build up a repertoire of opinions and a stock of standard ideas which can be churned out at a moment's notice. Even our religious beliefs can suffer the same treatment and we embrace or condemn doctrines which we have never bothered to consider.

The Bible is at pains to point out the fallibility of the human mind. The pagans who refused to honour God are said to be 'futile in their thinking' (Romans 1:21). Human insight can be misleading (Proverbs 3:5); certainly it cannot discover God unaided: 'In the wisdom of God, the world did not know God through wisdom' (1 Corinthians 1:21). As with the rest of the personality, the reason needs renewing; in a famous verse Paul puts the whole thing in a nutshell: 'Don't let the world around you squeeze you into its own mould, but let God re-mould your minds from within' (Romans 12:2, J. B. Phillips).

The Christian world-view starts with God and accepts his ultimate values and truths as universally applicable; the modern mind believes conversely that 'in philosophy as in logic, there are truths but no truth' :[3] in other words, what is, is right. Yet how often do Christians allow secular thinking to influence their attitudes to suffering, war, punishment of offenders, private enterprise, education, and even to the nature of God and the purpose of life! 'We must move with the times' is the motto of a mindless generation.

Of course, we can be pharisaical and exalt our petty preferences and secondary shibboleths above the plain principles of Scripture, and blind ourselves to further understanding. That is irrational thinking; that is giving emotional preference to error. In contrast to those whose 'heart has grown dull, and their ears ... heavy of hearing, and their eyes ... closed' (Matthew 13:15), we are to 'gird up' our minds (1 Peter 1:13). Instead of allowing politicians or preachers, writers or broadcasters, to do our thinking for us (although many of us could do with listening and reading more and propounding less), we are to learn how to handle the Word of truth correctly (2 Timothy 2:15). Then we can state our case with conviction mellowed by 'gentleness and reverence' (1 Peter 3:15) – which brings us to a still more personal and practical meaning of 'the heart'.

Sweet reasonableness

A. T. Schofield, in 1898, wrote what he claimed was the first English book on the unconscious mind. He had been shouted down by a learned society when he tried to read them a paper on the subject, and no doubt contemporary churchmen were a little perturbed, too; Dr Schofield was a committed Christian. Today, most of us have come to acknowledge that there are hidden thoughts and motives which influence our character.

It would be too trite to suggest that the Bible anticipated Messrs Freud, Adler and Jung by two thousand years, but it would none the less be true to say that it is well aware of the depths of the human heart.

'The inward mind and heart of a man are deep!' exclaims the psalmist (64:6), and the sage observes that 'as in water face answers to face, so the mind of man reflects the man' (Proverbs 27:19). This is so even during our sleeping hours; Jung described dreams as 'the natural reaction of the self-regulating psychic system',[4] and the Bible does not disagree. The contented lover slept, 'but my heart was awake', dreaming of her partner (Song of Solomon 5:2), while the anxious business man, whose 'days are full of pain', discovers that 'even in the night his mind does not rest' (Ecclesiastes 2:23). And, of course, the stress diseases to which we are so prone today point to the influence of the 'heart' and the body upon each other and thus emphasize the deeply rooted unity of the personality: 'A tranquil mind gives life to the flesh, but passion makes the bones rot' (Proverbs 14:30).

Jesus regarded the heart as the source of human behaviour. 'The good man out of the good treasure of his heart produces good, and the evil man out of his evil treasure produces evil; for out of the abundance of the heart his mouth speaks' (Luke 6:45). That outward responses betray inner resources is a recurring theme of Scripture. 'You will know them by their fruits,' said Jesus. 'Are grapes gathered from thorns, or figs from thistles? . . . A sound tree cannot bear evil fruit, nor can a bad tree bear good fruit' (Matthew 7:16, 18). James agrees: 'Does a spring pour forth from the same opening fresh water and brackish?' he asks (3:11).

Of course, you and I are very good at disguising the true state of our hearts by conforming to certain patterns of behaviour. We cover our insecurity or insincerity by adopting an 'in' language or life-style, but usually the little things let us down. The furtive eyes reveal that we are not nearly so interested in the person we are talking with as our 'Really?' and 'How interesting!' are meant to convey. The slip of the tongue or the unkept promise betrays a lack of commitment which we would verbally deny. And the feeble excuses for those unfulfilled intentions are a very thin mask covering an unpleasant truth: 'The heart is deceitful above all things, and desperately corrupt; who can understand it?' (Jeremiah 17:9).

The Bible reminds us that on the one hand our inner motives for seemingly good actions are often impure, while on the other hand the seemingly good intentions which do not result in action are little less than sheer lies. Jesus had no hesitation in endorsing Jeremiah's sombre conclusion; 'For from within, out of the heart of man, come evil thoughts, fornication, theft, murder, adultery, coveting, wickedness, deceit, licentiousness, envy, slander, pride, foolishness' (Mark 7:21f.). If you and I have not stolen, we have deceived; if we are not adulterous we are covetous. As with the rest of our human nature, the heart is not excluded from our fallen state.

One of the most tragic of all the heroes of literature faced this truth but knew of no solution to it. Sidney Carton, the brilliant law student, is portrayed by Charles Dickens in *A tale of two cities* as 'a man of good abilities and good emotions, incapable of their directed exercise, incapable of his own help and his own happiness, sensible of the blight upon him, and resigning himself to let it eat him away.'[5] But the Bible does not despair of the renewing of the heart; instead it looks forward to the day when you and I will be characterized by what Matthew Arnold, the nineteenth-century literary critic and liberal theologian, described as 'sweet reasonableness'.

'Sweet reasonableness' was how Arnold rendered a Greek word which is usually translated *gentleness*; 'The wisdom from above is first pure, then peaceable, *gentle*, open to reason, full of mercy and good fruits, without uncertainty or insincerity'

(James 3:17). A whole book could be written on that one verse; it is itself a commentary on 'sweet reasonableness'. It speaks of a God-given moderation which has reason and emotion in perfect balance and harmony; it is characterized by fairness and kindness in outward actions which spring from a heart that is both honest and righteous, a heart that is at peace with God.

It is, of course, no guarantee against pressures and problems, a kind of numbness that never feels the extremes of suffering or success. Indeed, it is a state of heightened sensitivity to human feelings, but one which is matched by a deepened trust in the love and power of God. 'A new heart will I give you, and a new spirit I will put within you; and I will take out of your flesh the heart of stone and give you a heart of flesh' (Ezekiel 36:26).

Yet again we have a glimpse of the biblical promise of a renewed and restored humanity (we will look at it in detail in chapter 9). But before we do that, we must shift our position once more; the scriptural painting of human nature has not yet revealed all its truths about the inner workings of the personality. We must discover precisely what Ezekiel – and other writers – meant by the words 'flesh' and 'spirit'; they are crucial – and often very confusing.

And to do that we turn from the sad figure of Sidney Carton to the even more tragic and horrifying literary figure of Dr Henry Jekyll. Or is it Mr Edward Hyde?

Follow-up

1. How do the various usages of the word 'heart' relate to one another? (All these verses have 'heart' in the original, even if the English translation uses 'mind' or something similar.) Numbers 24:13; 1 Samuel 24:5; 2 Samuel 6:16; Psalms 12:2; 62:10; 95:8; Proverbs 13:12; Isaiah 29:13; Mark 6:52; Luke 1:66; Acts 16:14; Romans 6:17; Colossians 3:22.

2. What do these verses tell us about the nature and importance

of the mind? Nehemiah 8:13; Psalms 82:5; 139:2; Isaiah 1:18; Hosea 4:6; Luke 24:45; Acts 17:2; 2 Corinthians 10:5; Ephesians 4:18; 1 Thessalonians 2:2; 2 Timothy 3:8.

3. What can you find in the Bible to help you understand and cope with your emotions? Joshua 1:6–9; Psalm 119:11; Matthew 6:25–34 (*cf.* 1 Timothy 5:8); Philippians 4:4–9 (*cf.* John 14:27).

References

[1] G. Abbott-Smith, *A Manual Greek lexicon of the New Testament* (T. and T. Clark, 1937), definition of *kardia*.

[2] Terence Rattigan, *In praise of love* (Hamish Hamilton, 1973), p. 51.

[3] Albert Camus, *The myth of Sisyphus* (Hamish Hamilton, 1955), p. 22.

[4] C. C. Jung, *Analytical psychology* (Routledge and Kegan Paul, 1968), p. 124.

[5] Charles Dickens, *A tale of two cities* (Cassell, 1907), p. 92.

'On almost every occasion when I have met somebody, I have met somebody else. That is, I have met a private man who was oddly different from the public man.'
(G. K. Chesterton)

'When I looked into the mirror, I shrieked, and my heart throbbed: for not myself did I see therein, but a devil's grimace and derision.'
(Nietzsche)

8

Dr Jekyll and Mr Hyde

Robert Louis Stevenson's classic story *The strange case of Dr Jekyll and Mr Hyde* is about a respectable family doctor who, like all of us, is acutely aware of a conflict within his own personality. On the one hand he is conscious of what he *ought* to do; on the other hand he finds that he *wants* to do something quite different. But he is not two different people inside one skin; 'Of the two natures that contended in the field of my consciousness, even if I could rightly be said to be either, it was only because I was radically both.'[1] He is determined to try to separate these natures so that he can be either wholly good without being constantly dragged down by his 'lower self', or wholly bad without possessing a trace of conscience.

Anticipating the users of LSD in our own generation he prepares a drug which will liberate his mind. He drinks down the potion, convulses, and finds that the well-intentioned Dr Henry Jekyll has turned into the evil-faced Mr Edward Hyde. Jekyll takes a liking to Hyde: 'This, too, was myself. It seemed natural and human. In my eyes it bore a livelier image of the spirit, it seemed more express and single, than the imperfect and divided countenance I had hitherto been accustomed to call mine.'[2] Hyde, however, has no interest at all in the scruples of Jekyll; he is 'a being inherently malign and villainous; his every act and thought centred on self; drinking pleasure with bestial avidity . . . relentless like a man of stone.'[3]

Jekyll is able to slip from one personality to the other with ease for a while. He is supremely confident that Jekyll can control Hyde; 'The moment I choose I can be rid of Mr Hyde,' he tells a friend.[4] Slowly, however, Hyde begins to overpower the doctor. He murders an innocent passer-by in cold blood, and Jekyll, overcome with remorse, assures his friend that Hyde 'will never more be heard of'.[5]

For two months he keeps his word: he keeps off the drugs and Hyde to all intents and purposes has disappeared off the face of the earth. But Jekyll's repentance is short-lived; the lure of Hyde's loose life is too powerful for the doctor to resist. When the public outcry has died down, he turns himself into the murderer once more. This time, however, there is no turning back. Jekyll soon finds that he can become Hyde without the drugs, and that he now needs them constantly to retain his own identity. As his irreplaceable supply of chemicals runs short, his body and mind degenerate, and after writing his confessions he dies in the emaciated and grotesque form of Mr Edward Hyde.

Whatever Stevenson's intentions when writing the story, he has provided us with a parable. The Bible also speaks of two principles in the human personality. It calls one the 'spirit'; it is like Dr Jekyll. The other it calls the 'flesh', which is like Mr Hyde. The parallel will become clearer as we see what the Bible means by each of these terms.

The spirit is willing . . .

Most books about human nature have some reference to the 'spirit'. The word usually describes the non-physical aspects of our personality, our ability to think and feel, to reflect upon the past and to rise above our present circumstances. Sometimes, 'spirit' designates the sources of human creativity or the centre of religious consciousness.

Whenever the Bible refers to man's spirit, it means all these things and more. The 'soul' is man seen as a living person; the 'heart' is man viewed in terms of his inner consciousness. *The 'spirit' is man in God's image described from the angle of the nature or quality of his personal life.* But as with all these words, 'spirit' has several shades of meaning and overlaps other terms.

The biblical word is also used for 'wind' or breath. In Ezekiel's vision of the valley of dry bones, the translators have difficulty in choosing between the words. 'Then he said to me, "Prophesy to the breath (or wind or spirit) . . . Thus says the Lord God: Come from the four winds, O breath (or wind or spirit), and breathe upon these slain, that they may live"' (37:9). This passage uses 'spirit' to mean 'the principle of life', that which animates a corpse. 'The body apart from the spirit is dead' (James 2:26). Life is not something which can exist in its own right, but is a quality of animal or vegetable existence endowed by the Creator who values and 'yearns jealously over the spirit which he has made to dwell in us' (James 4:5). There is no warrant in Scripture for thinking of the dead as 'spirits'* although it has been suggested that the pains of hell are due in part to the bodiless state of its inmates; they are disembodied spirits suffering the anguish of incompleteness. Hence we are given no encouragement in the Bible to think of 'spirit' as some*thing* which dwells within us. Today, we would use the phrase 'my life' as the ancients used 'my spirit'. We have no control over this life; we can assemble its components but we cannot truly create it, nor can we retain it. 'No man has power to retain the spirit, or authority over the day of death' (Ecclesiastes 8:8).

We do have some say over the quality of our life, however. The pharaoh who persistently refused to grant Moses' request to 'let my people go' had a hardened spirit (Exodus 7:14); we would say that he was a hard man. Nebuchadnezzar, after a

* The only possible exception to this rule is in Hebrews 12:23 which speaks of 'the spirits of just men made perfect'. As we have seen, the Bible teaches the resurrection of the whole man after death; the context of this verse seems to be that of Old Testament believers before the final resurrection.

particularly bad dream, had a troubled spirit (Daniel 2:1); he was a worried man. It was said of Caleb, who in contrast to his friends with whom he spied out the promised land was faithful to God, 'My servant Caleb ... has a different spirit and has followed me fully' (Numbers 14:24). In other words, Caleb had a different attitude to things; the orientation of his personality and the nature of his character were quite unlike that of the others.

This meaning of 'spirit' is made clearer by a statement of Paul's. He tells the Corinthians that although he is physically absent he is 'present in spirit' (1 Corinthians 5:3). Paul is neither claiming psychic powers nor uttering pious platitudes; he is saying that he is thinking of them and praying for them, that he is concerned for their welfare, and missing their fellowship. You and I know something of how Paul felt in his spirit; when we are absent from a friend or a group with whom we identify, there wells up within us a longing to be with them and to share in their activities, and in our imagination we go to them and stand beside them: our whole being is oriented towards them.

There is a similar experience when we put everything we have into something, and we become completely caught up in what we are doing. Back in chapter two I mentioned Vaslav Nijinsky, the ballet dancer. Those who saw him were impressed not only by his technical excellence, but also by his ability to interpret the characters he danced. On stage, Nijinsky disappeared and the ethereal Spirit of the Rose or the sad clown Petrushka took his place. His spirit, his whole life, was for those few minutes totally oriented towards the person he portrayed.

In the Bible, it is God who is seen as being supremely worthy of this quality of devotion and commitment. Paul, who claimed to serve God with his spirit (Romans 1:9), showed through his life that serving was a matter of commitment expressed by action: 'For to me to live is Christ, and to die is gain' (Philippians 1:21). When Isaiah wrote, 'My spirit within me earnestly seeks thee' (26:9), he meant that his whole being longed for the presence and power of God. Jesus told us to worship God 'in spirit and truth' (John 4:24). Paul prayed with his spirit (1 Corinthians 14:14); in these contexts Jesus and Paul do not mean 'with the aid of the Holy Spirit' (we are told elsewhere that this, too, is an element of worship) but 'without reserve'. Instead of singing the hymn and thinking about the lunch in the oven, we are to sing the praises of him who is the centre of our attention and the focus of our thoughts.

Too frequently, though, our spirits are taken up more with the lunch than with the Lord, and even then we are rather apathetic. (I almost wrote, 'half-hearted'; I said that the words overlapped!) At the very best, our spirit is no different from the character of Dr Jekyll, 'an incongruous compound of whose reformation and improvement I had . . . learned to despair.'[6] We see that compound in other people every day; the telephonist who is sweet-tempered and charming to a customer is sour and contentious with a colleague. We see that compound in ourselves every hour as we do good only to those who do good to us. 'What credit is that to you?' asked Jesus. 'For even sinners do the same . . . But love your enemies, and do good, and lend, expecting nothing in return; and your reward will be great, and you will be sons of the most High, for he is kind to the ungrateful and selfish' (Luke 6:33, 35).

You and I know that it is quite impossible for us to keep Jesus' command consistently; and he and many other people in the Bible knew it too. That is why the need for inner renewal is so strongly emphasized. 'A new heart will I give you, and a new spirit I will put within you . . . and cause you to walk in my statutes and be careful to observe my ordinances' (Ezekiel 36:26f.). A new source of action, a new attitude of spirit: both made possible by the penetration of the Holy Spirit into the human heart and spirit. And only that penetration of God's

Spirit can deal adequately with that undesirable alien, the flesh: 'If you live according to the flesh you will die, but if by the spirit you put to death the deeds of the body you will live. For all who are led by the Spirit of God are sons of God' (Romans 8:13f.).

. . . but the flesh is weak

The word 'flesh' is used in Scripture, as in common speech, to signify the bodily tissue; in Ezekiel's vision in the valley, God says to the skeletons: 'I will lay sinews upon you, and will cause flesh to come upon you' (37:6). It can mean the meat of animals; the quails eaten by the Israeli refugees in the desert are called 'flesh' (Exodus 16:6ff.). Mankind is collectively referred to as flesh in Isaiah 40:5: 'The glory of the Lord shall be revealed, and all flesh shall see it together.'

But the passage which follows that verse points to the most significant meaning of the word. 'All flesh is grass, and all its beauty is like the flower of the field . . . The grass withers, the flower fades; but the word of our God will stand for ever' (Isaiah 40:6, 8). '*Flesh*' *is man seen in terms of his natural limitations and weaknesses.* In comparison with God it is puny and ineffective: 'With him is an arm of flesh; but with us is the Lord our God' was king Hezekiah's estimate of the Assyrian threat to Jerusalem (2 Chronicles 32:8). In his dealings with men, God remembers that they are but flesh, and is therefore patient and compassionate (Psalm 78:38f.). And Paul, explaining the effects of Christ's 'new management' of a person's life when they become a Christian, says, 'I am speaking in human terms, because of your natural limitations' (literally, 'because of your flesh', Romans 6:19).

It is Paul who gives the word its full ethical meaning; on several occasions he makes uncompromising statements like, 'Those who are in the flesh cannot please God' (Romans 8:8), and, 'The desires of the flesh are against the Spirit' (Galatians 5:17). Paul is not, of course, thinking of the physical body; there is a clear distinction between it and the flesh in his teaching. 'The body can become the instrument of the service and glory of God; the flesh cannot. The body can be purified and even glorified; the flesh must be eliminated and eradicated.'[7]

Paul uses 'flesh' in a similar way to 'world';* on one occasion the translators have put 'world' where the Greek has 'flesh'. 'Some . . . suspect us of acting in worldly fashion (according to the flesh). For though we live in the world (walk after the flesh) we are not carrying on a worldly war (fighting according to the flesh), for the weapons of our warfare are not worldly (fleshly) but have divine power to destroy strongholds' (2 Corinthians 10:2–4). *Flesh in this sense means individual human life organized in opposition, or without reference, to God.* It is fallen man as he naturally is, enclosed within his own self-interest; it is 'his sinful propensity inherited from Adam'.[8] 'If you live according to the flesh', says Paul, 'you will die' (Romans 8:13).

In his list of the works of the flesh, Paul makes it quite clear that mental attitudes and spiritual apostasies are as 'fleshly' as physical abuses: 'Fornication, impurity, licentiousness, idolatry, sorcery, enmity, strife, jealousy, anger, selfishness, dissension, party spirit, envy, drunkenness, carousing, and the like' (Galatians 5:19ff.). The Mr Hyde inside each one of us enjoys instant gratification of his desires and expects instant justice in his relationships; he looks for a self-indulgent life that is as easy and simple to lead as his instant coffee is to make. He equates a sense of physical and mental well-being with the highest good without caring (or daring) to lift his eyes above the ground lest a higher (and harder) principle of life should confront him.

On the occasions when he is so confronted, he finds himself back in the shoes of Dr Jekyll. 'Strange as my circumstances were,' he wrote, 'the terms of this debate are as old and

* See chapter 5 for a discussion of the biblical use of 'world'.

commonplace as man; much the same inducements and charms cast the die for any tempted and trembling sinner; and it fell out with me, as it falls out with so vast a majority of my fellows, that I chose the better part and was found wanting in the strength to keep it.'[9]

'The spirit indeed is willing, but the flesh is weak' were the words of Jesus as he faced the greatest temptation of his life in the garden of Gethsemane (Matthew 26:41). To endure the pain and despise the shame, or to preserve his life: that was the question. The spirit rises to the challenge; the flesh retreats from the inconvenience. The spirit is willing to fight; the flesh wishes only to relax. And that brings us to the heart of the battle Paul wrote so much about.

And the race is not yet over

The Christian and the athlete have one thing in common: their worst enemy. Christopher Brasher, a former champion runner, wrote:

> A distance runner's greatest enemy is himself: the weakness of his body, the friability of his will. He trains both until he knows that neither will collapse. There are days of bodily weakness, but never can the will be allowed to feel sorry for the physical man, never can it give way.[10]

The weakness of the flesh and the fallenness of the spirit, 'the sin which clings so closely', hinder us from running 'with perseverance the race that is set before us' (Hebrews 12:1). The New Testament holds out no promise of a Christian life which is like a permanent holiday in the sunshine. 'Forgetting what lies behind and straining forward to what lies ahead,' Paul wrote to the Philippians, 'I press on toward the goal for the prize of the upward call of God in Christ Jesus' (3:13f.). The word 'straining' is used in Greek of athletes throwing every effort into the final sprint up the home straight, lungs bursting, heart pounding, muscles aching. Writing to the Corinthians he says, 'I do not run aimlessly, I do not box as one beating the air; but I pommel my body and subdue it, lest after preaching to others I myself should be disqualified' (1 Corinthians 9:26f.). The word 'pommel' is a boxing term for giving someone a black eye; 'subdue' literally means 'enslave'. The Christian needs to be as personally fit and disciplined for serving Christ as the athlete needs to be for a top competition. There is a fight to be won against the forces of evil; there is a marathon to be run in which the flesh and the spirit are competing.

That conflict is increased rather than decreased when a person becomes a Christian. He is no longer merely that incongruous compound of Dr Jekyll; a distortion of the image of God too weak to do other than follow the dictates of the flesh. A new principle of life has been implanted within him; he has a new ethical orientation. 'You are not in the flesh,' Paul writes to the believers in Rome, 'you are in the Spirit, if in fact the Spirit of God dwells in you. Any one who does not have the Spirit of Christ does not belong to him' (Romans 8:9). *The Christian's new spirit is God's Spirit, and God's Spirit is holy.*

In other words, the conflict is not between two opposing segments of the human personality; the Holy Spirit heals divisions, he does not create them. Rather, it is between fallen man and the Spirit of God who is working to bring our nature into conformity with his. 'For the desires of the flesh are against the Spirit, and the desires of the Spirit are against the flesh; for these are opposed to each other, to prevent you from doing what you would' (Galatians 5:17).

The Christian is a citizen of two worlds. He belongs to the kingdom of this world by birth and natural inclination; he lives in it still and shares in the weaknesses, limitations and fallenness of human flesh. But he is also a citizen of the kingdom of God by inheritance and spiritual inclination; he already shares in something of its life, and its standards are already a powerful influence upon him. He is like a compass needle drawn towards God but deflected by outside influences ('the world') and his own sinful desires ('the flesh'). Like Dr Doolittle's two-headed pushme-pullyou, he is being dragged in two directions at once: 'I delight in the law of God, in my inmost self, but I see in my members another law at war with the law of my mind and making me captive to the law of sin which dwells in my members' (Romans 7:22f.).*

Dr Jekyll has been given a new orientation of life; a new managing director has taken over the crumbling firm and given it a new dynamic and ethos. But Mr Hyde is still lurking in the background, 'drinking pleasure with bestial avidity', seeming 'natural and human', and possessing 'a livelier image of the spirit' than Jekyll. The Christian does not lose his humanness when the Spirit of God takes charge of him; he is still 'radically both' Jekyll and Hyde. But Hyde is now under sentence of death.

'We know that our old self was crucified with (Jesus) so that the sinful body might be destroyed, and we might no longer be enslaved to sin' (Romans 6:6). 'Those who belong to Christ Jesus have crucified the flesh with its passions and desires' (Galatians 5:24). The power of the flesh to keep you and me

* Romans 7:14-25 has been the centre of considerable theological controversy. Paul's strong language ('I am . . . sold under sin;' 'I can will what is right, but I cannot do it') is held by some to apply to his pre-conversion experience; it seems incompatible with the Christian victory and triumph over sin of which he speaks elsewhere. The note of victory is not, however, absent from this passage (verse 25), and Paul would never claim that a non-Christian could *delight* in God's law; that is an effect of the Holy Spirit's renewing work. In any case, he uses the present tense in these verses, having been speaking of his pre-conversion experience *in the past tense* in verses 1–13. His comments here seem to back up what he says elsewhere, but because of the dispute I have drawn most of my references from Romans 6 and 8, and Galatians 5, about which there is no doubt.

from knowing God was broken by Jesus Christ. When a person becomes a Christian it is as if he nails his old nature, his flesh, to the cross, and receives in its place a new nature, the Holy Spirit, to be his ethical standard and strength. *But every time Paul says, 'You have died,' he also says, 'You must go on dying.'*

'Do not yield your members to sin as instruments of wickedness, but yield . . . your members to God as instruments of righteousness' (Romans 6:13). 'Do not use your freedom as an opportunity for the flesh . . . but I say, walk by the Spirit, and do not gratify the desires of the flesh' (Galatians 5:13, 16). The fallenness of his human nature can *still* be the dominant influence upon a Christian's life. The flesh is totally incompatible with the Holy Spirit; but it is not impossible to indulge it. The lure of Hyde's loose life is always a powerful one. The brashness of a Jekyll who boasts 'I can be rid of Hyde any moment I choose' is quickly replaced by the lame excuse, 'I'm only human,' when he gives in to Hyde's pressure, which is often as subtle as it is strong. The Bible is not unaware of the pleasures of sin, but it says they are fleeting (Hebrews 11:25). There are other pleasures which are permanent and pure, because they are centred on Christ and characterized by righteousness.

But if sin is not impossible for a Christian, neither is it inevitable. God is 'able to keep you from falling' (Jude 24) and 'will not let you be tempted beyond your strength, but with the temptation will also provide the way of escape, that you may be able to endure it' (1 Corinthians 10:13). The victory has already been won, but guerrilla skirmishes continue. We are to enter into the victory by 'walking by the Spirit'; unfortunately Hyde's influence is such that we do not always even wish to.

The first great secret of holiness lies in the degree and decisiveness of our repentance. If besetting sins persistently plague us, it is either because we have never truly repented, or because, having repented, we have not maintained our repentance. It is as if, having nailed our old nature to the cross, we keep wistfully returning to the scene of its execution. We begin to fondle it, to caress it, to long for its release, even to try to take it down again from the cross. We need to learn to leave it there. When some jealous, or proud, or malicious, or impure thought invades our mind we must kick it out at once. It is fatal to begin to examine it and consider whether we are going to give in to it or not. We have declared war on it; we are not going to resume negotiations. We have settled the issue for good; we are not going to re-open it. We have crucified the flesh, we are never going to draw the nails.[11]

In the story, Jekyll never 'crucified' Hyde and he never received the new Spirit which alone could provide the answer for which he searched. His repentance was therefore doomed to failure; 'In my case, to be tempted, however slightly, was to fall.'[12] He is a Canute trying to be the Creator; he seeks to stem the tide of human sinfulness but his only tool is his own human sinfulness. He is an Egyptian horseman charging across the Red Sea without faith in Israel's God. And the tide rises above him; the waters roll forward and engulf him. Without God's Spirit, the flesh is unconquerable and the human spirit impotent. Stevenson's novel provides a salutary warning to all of us who are genuinely concerned about the quality of human life.

But for all the reality he expresses, the two-in-one personality of Dr Jekyll is a creation of fiction. The person who dominates the next chapter had a real life that in some ways seems stranger than fiction. Instead of giving in to temptation with ease, he resisted it totally, to the point of death. Instead of being plagued with an incongruous mixture of good intentions and evil actions he was a person whom his enemies and his friends both attested as being without sin. In the words of Martin Luther, he is 'the proper man'; he is the example of what you and I should be, and he is, paradoxically, also the means of our becoming what we shall be.

Follow-up

1. Build up a more comprehensive understanding of the meanings of 'flesh' and 'spirit' by looking up the following references. How are the words used? What can you learn about your own life from them?

a. *The flesh*: Genesis 6:3; Psalm 84:2; Jeremiah 32:27; Joel 2:28; John 3:6; 17:2; Galatians 2:19f.; Colossians 2:23.

b. *The spirit*: Numbers 5:13f.; Job 7:11; Proverbs 11:13; Ecclesiastes 11:5; 12:7; Isaiah 57:15; Matthew 5:3; Mark 8:12; Acts 17:16; 1 Corinthians 4:21; 2 Timothy 1:7.

2. Read Galatians chapters 5 and 6. Note every occurrence of 'flesh' or 'spirit', and put Paul's statements into your own words. Note especially each of the works of the flesh and the fruit of the Spirit: what do they really mean? A dictionary may help, and if you have access to a good basic commentary (*e.g. The new Bible commentary revised*, or John Stott, *Only one way*, both published by IVP) use it to supplement and check your own conclusions.

References

[1] Robert Louis Stevenson, *The strange case of Dr Jekyll and Mr Hyde* (Eveleigh Nash and Grayson, n.d.), pp. 114f.

[2] *op. cit.*, p. 120.

[3] *op. cit.*, p. 125.

[4] *op. cit.*, p. 35.

[5] *op. cit.*, p. 49.

[6] *op. cit.*, p. 122.

[7] William Barclay, *Flesh and spirit* (SCM, 1962), p. 20.

[8] F. F. Bruce, *Romans* (IVP, 1963), p. 43.

[9] Stevenson, *op. cit.*, p. 132.

[10] Christopher Brasher in *The Observer*, 3 August 1975.

[11] John Stott, *The message of Galatians* (IVP, 1968), pp. 151f. (This book has since been re-issued with the title *Only one way*.)

[12] Stevenson, *op. cit.*, p. 134.

'*The superhuman is the only place where you can find the human.*'
(G. K. Chesterton)

'*Only in novels does one change condition or become better.*'
(Albert Camus)

9
Metamorphosis

Every mountain has its peak. Sometimes the summit is visible from many miles away, and however far we walk towards it, it never seems any nearer. Sometimes it is hidden by lower peaks and slopes, so that we clamber on in faith, knowing that it exists but seeing it only when we are almost on top of it.

In all the chapters of this book we have had glimpses of the human summit; that renewed human nature which the Bible promises to those who follow Jesus Christ. We have had to cover a great deal of ground before tackling the peak itself; the path towards it is long and narrow, but it is clearly marked. Ahead of us has gone someone in whose footsteps we can follow, and beside us travels an astute guide and an amenable companion.

The proper man

Jesus Christ is an enigmatic figure whom the world just cannot forget. His birth is celebrated across the globe, and even though we have largely secularized Christmas, our calendar still dates from the time when an extraordinary child was born into the warm dampness of a Palestinian cow shed. Jesus has been portrayed on stage as a jovial clown and on screen as a defeated idealist; he has been championed as a revolutionary and condemned as a reactionary. Yet in every generation the quality of his life and the claims of his teaching have come as a renewed challenge to human conduct and to the individual conscience.

Little is known about his early life. He was the eldest of at least seven children and helped to provide for them by working in the family building and joinery business (Mark 6:3). He never married, but had no difficulty in relating to women. He was quite indifferent to the materialistic standards of his day; he owned no house (Luke 9:58) and had no savings with which to pay the statutory taxes (Matthew 17:24–27).

But he none the less did pay his taxes, and he refused to lead an insurrection against the occupying power. He displayed intense anger at the sacrilegious trading within the temple precincts (John 2:14ff.) but forbade the use of force to resist his unlawful arrest (John 18:11). He trod the knife-edge path of rejecting the traditions of the scribes whilst retaining the teachings of the Old Testament Scriptures: 'I have not come to abolish (the law and the prophets) . . . but to fulfil them' (Matthew 5:17).

He maintained the same balance in his emotional and physical life. His opponents called him mad (John 10:20), yet he remained cool even under intense emotional and physical pressure. He had the presence of mind, while hanging in agony on the cross, to commit the care and protection of his mother to one of his closest friends (John 19:26f.). He never seems to have had unpleasant or unrealistic thoughts; but on the contrary he was always patient with people and addressed their immediate needs. He was never moody (although at times seems to have become a little dejected by his faithless disciples), and he never did bizarre things; many of his miracles were performed quietly and unobtrusively, and never to order. He was physically tough enough to go without food for six weeks in the extreme temperatures of the south Judaean desert (Matthew 4:2), but he was not a muscle-bound he-man, unable to feel his own weakness or to feel for the weakness of others. He cried when his friend died (John 11:35) and suffered intense emotional strain shortly before his betrayal (Mark 13:33ff.), yet during his trial he remained patient and composed. In a word, he was the embodiment of 'sweet reasonableness'.

He always had time for people. He gave his full attention to the humblest widow and the wealthiest official; he was as at home in a hovel as he was at a dinner party. People in their thousands downed tools and trekked out into the market place or grazing-grounds to sit and listen to him for hours and even days at a time. 'And they were astonished at his teaching, for he taught them as one who had authority, and not as the scribes' (Mark 1:22).

The teaching of Jesus has astonished men and women ever since. On the one hand he held out the highest, noblest and most difficult ethic the world has ever known: 'You, therefore, must be perfect, as your heavenly Father is perfect' (Matthew 5:48). That perfection included the inner attitude as well as the outward action. He turned the rough justice of the world upside down in the command, 'Love your enemies and pray for those who persecute you' (Matthew 5:44). At his own trial, he practised what he preached. On the other hand, he offered forgiveness to those who had failed to keep God's standards, and the harshness of condemnation was on his lips only when he faced the rank hypocrisy of those who could not see their own sinfulness. And therein lies the rub.

'Why does this man speak thus? It is blasphemy! Who can forgive sins but God alone?' (Mark 2:7). Jesus' teaching about God cannot be detached from his teaching about human behaviour; and his claim to be God in human form, to be an utterly unique revelation of God, cannot be divorced from the perfection of his life. However hard we try, we cannot remove the feeding of the multitude, the walking on the water, and especially the resurrection, from the biblical narrative without destroying its unity and desecrating its message.

Certainly we can look back to Jesus Christ and see a model life which we would do well to follow. Peter, one of Jesus' closest companions, wrote: 'Christ also suffered for you, leaving you an example, that you should follow in his steps. He committed no sin; no guile was found on his lips' (1 Peter 2:21f.). Paul tells us that Jesus is 'the image of the invisible God' (Colossians 1:15); in other words, the embodiment of what you and I, people made in the image of God, should be.

But Paul does not stop there, nor does Peter, nor can you and I. Paul expands on what he means by 'the image of God' as applied to Jesus: 'In him all the fullness of God was pleased to dwell, and through him to reconcile to himself all things . . . making peace by the blood of his cross' (Colossians 1:19f.). Jesus, it has been said, was born to die. We cannot deny that he himself saw his death as an *effective* end to his ministry: 'For the Son of man also came not to be served but to serve, and to give his life as a ransom for many' (Mark 10:45). And the whole New Testament looks to the blackest day of human history, when the only truly human person who has ever lived was ruthlessly executed on trumped-up charges – and we call it *Good* Friday, because it spells hope for you and me. 'For Christ also died for sins once for all, the righteous for the unrighteous, that he might bring us to God' (1 Peter 3:18).

The proemial man*

A former professional golfer once told me that he would get up each morning and decide who he would be and what characteristics he would adopt for that day, in order to be a better person and player. The desire to be someone different is a universal symptom of the fallenness of mankind; we are all conscious that we are not who and what we should be. We speak of turning over a new leaf, of realizing our potential, of making new year's resolutions, but fundamentally we remain

* *Proem:* an introduction, preamble, preface, prelude.

the same people inside. American writer Charles Reich sees a new attitude to life emerging today; he calls it 'Consciousness III', and admits that a long period of education is required if it is ever to catch on.[1] And a British commentator observes that 'Ideal societies cannot be made with imperfect people';[2] man's dreams of the future have always been frustrated by human failings.

As we have seen in the previous chapters, the Bible writers agree that people need changing; but the method of change which they suggest is quite unique. They do not emphasize educational or environmental factors, nor do they bow before evolutionary forces. Instead, they propose a complete transformation of the whole inner being of a person, a *metamorphosis*. A metamorphosis is an irreversible change of one substance into another. Marble is metamorphosed limestone; pastry is metamorphosed flour and fat; a butterfly is a metamorphosed caterpillar. 'Do not be conformed to this world', writes Paul, 'but be transformed (literally, metamorphosed) by the renewal of your mind' (Romans 12:2). 'We . . . are being changed (literally, metamorphosed) into his likeness from one degree of glory into another' (2 Corinthians 3:18). The image of God is being restored to its true nature as the Christian is transformed by God's renewing Spirit. 'If any one is in Christ, he is a new creation; the old has passed away, behold, the new has come' (2 Corinthians 5:17).

Through our village there runs a bourn, an intermittent stream. One day, a few years ago, it suddenly dried up, and one day, just as suddenly, it started flowing again. For months the water trickled over the mud and stones, until gradually a few water plants began to grow and fronds of weed waved in the current. Months more passed, until one day I saw a tiny fish: the river had come alive.

The transforming power of God is often likened to water in Scripture. 'O God, thou art my God, I seek thee, my soul thirsts for thee . . . as in a dry and weary land where no water is' (Psalm 63:1). 'Blessed is the man who trusts in the Lord . . . he is like a tree planted by water, that sends out its roots by the stream, and does not fear when heat comes, for its leaves remain green' (Jeremiah 17:7f.). 'Jesus stood up and proclaimed, "If any one thirst, let him come to me and drink. He who believes in me, as the scripture has said, 'Out of his heart shall flow rivers of living water.' " Now this he said of the Spirit, which those who believed in him were to receive' (John 7:37ff.).

The essence of the Christian metamorphosis is the bestowal by God of a new principle of life, a new dynamic, upon the individual. This is not the realization of some latent powers nor the discovery of some divine spark within ourselves. We become alive to our Creator in a totally new way. 'And you he made alive, when you were dead through the trespasses and sins in which you once walked' (Ephesians 2:1f.). Instead of being alienated from our Maker we are reconciled to him (2 Corinthians 5:18). Jesus called this new harmony between God and man 'eternal life': 'And this is eternal life, that they know thee the only true God, and Jesus Christ whom thou hast sent,' he said (John 17:3).

All kinds of ideas have been floated about the nature of Christianity. There is the heresy that being a Christian is a matter of personal kindness and generosity. Pelagius, the monk I referred to in chapter two, started that one; man, he said, has the ability to live a Christian life without a change of heart. Then there is the common church illusion that a Christian is a person who performs certain duties or enjoys certain experiences. The New Testament rejects all these ideas, 'for neither circumcision counts for anything, nor uncircumcision, but a new creation' (Galatians 6:15). In other words, important as good conduct and spiritual experiences are, only a renewed relationship with God makes you a Christian. And without

140

that renewed relationship, there can be no renewed humanity, for man is made in the image of God.

From the human point of view, the restoration of the distorted image begins with the realization that restoration is necessary, that we are 'separated from Christ . . . having no hope and without God in the world' (Ephesians 2:12). From God's point of view, it began when he 'so loved the world that he gave his only Son, that whoever believes in him should not perish but have eternal life' (John 3:16). The New Testament writers never allow us to forget that man's alienation from God is such that only God himself can deal with it; nor will they allow us to look at God's method of dealing with it – the death and resurrection of Jesus Christ – and remain unmoved. God's Spirit, we are told, is at work within the world convicting people of their sinfulness, convincing them of the efficacy of Christ's death, and drawing them into what can only be described as a personal relationship with the Father (John 6:37; 14:8ff.). To believe is more than to acknowledge a creed; it is to admit the truth about ourselves and about God which the Bible reveals, and then to follow the living Jesus wherever he leads.

And at that point we are alive; we have been born again (John 3:3); the stream has begun to flow. 'You have put off the old nature with its practices and have put on the new nature, which is being renewed in knowledge after the image of its creator' (Colossians 3:9f.). Like the defector or emigré who abandons the country of his birth and seeks asylum in an adopted land, so we have turned our backs on the godless past and have been adopted by God into his kingdom. 'You are no longer strangers and sojurners, but you are fellow citizens with the saints and members of the household of God' (Ephesians 2:19).

My friend the golfer now knows who he is: a new creature in Christ. He no longer has to try on a new mask every day, but he does still have a struggle relating his new-found faith to the cut-throat business world in which he now works. The young student I mentioned in chapter three has come through her valley of doubt and uncertainty; she went into it already a Christian. We were granted a new nature and a new identity when we became Christians, but it may take some time and some difficulty before the metamorphosis takes effect or becomes apparent. It will certainly take a lifetime before it is complete. But all the while the Spirit of God is gently making his presence felt.

Every river bed is different. Some are rocky and others muddy. Some rivers will support trout while others can only manage tiddlers; lilies will grow beside some and rushes beside others. Just as we have no scientific justification for demanding that all rivers be alike, so we have no scriptural justification for demanding that all Christians should be alike, or that they should be instantly perfect. As C. S. Lewis once put it,

Who knows how much more cantankerous the old maid might be if she were *not* a Christian, and how much more likable the nice young fellow might be if he *were* a Christian? You can't judge Christianity simply by comparing the *product* in those two people; you would need to know what kind of raw material Christ was working on in both cases.[3]

In other words, God respects our individual personalities and takes us just as we are; he sets to work re-moulding the image this way in you and that way in me. Of course, we should both be growing in our experience of God's presence, guidance and help. We should be continually learning to 'put off the old nature which belongs to your former manner of life and is corrupt through deceitful lusts' - Mr Hyde dies hard, remember - 'and be renewed in the spirit of your minds, and put on the new nature, created after the likeness of God in true righteousness and holiness' (Ephesians 4:22ff.). This is no repetition of the new-leaf syndrome or the away-with-convention-and-be-yourself convention within which so many of our contemporaries are trapped; this is the active co-operation of you and me with our ever-present, always scrupulously honest, companion, guide and helper, the Holy Spirit. Listen to a former delinquent describe his post-conversion experience:

As I was Christianized so I was civilized. I cleaned my teeth; stopped swearing; said please and thank you. And there was a desire to learn. It all came from within, not forced from without. A new inner urge dictated effort for the best. I was not trying to conform to a type, for I had always suspected that the Christian gentleman was a play actor – manners being arbitrary![4]

Now listen to Paul as he describes the results of God's working within our lives. 'The fruit of the Spirit is love, joy, peace, patience, kindness, goodness, faithfulness, gentleness, self-control; against such there is no law . . . If we live by the Spirit' (*i.e.* if we have been made alive to God) 'let us also walk by the Spirit' (Galatians 5:22f., 25). And if that makes you feel very small and rather grubby and quite useless, remember Paul's assessment of his own life: 'Not that I . . . am already perfect . . . but one thing I do, forgetting what lies behind and straining forward to what lies ahead, I press on toward the goal for the prize of the upward call of God in Christ Jesus' (Philippians 3:12ff.). We are the proemial people, you and I; what we are now is but an introduction to what we shall be in the future.

The promised man

'*I teach you the Superman:* Man is something that is to be surpassed.'[5] Thus spake Friedrich Nietzsche, and his Superman was a ruthless demon who trampled over the weak and power-less. Men have often dreamt of a completely new race or class of humans, but the dream has usually been either a nightmare or a romantic illusion. Aldous Huxley peopled his *Brave new world* with battery-hatched creatures genetically and psycho-logically preconditioned to become morons or masters. Popular imagery has conjured up the god-like figures of James Bond, Dr Who and the Invisible Man, who exercise suprahuman powers in their fight for good against evil.

The New Testament also looks forward to the time when God will re-create our broken humanity and will establish 'a new heaven and a new earth in which righteousness dwells' (2 Peter 3:13). We are given two reasons why this vision is not just another empty promise or fanciful hope.

To begin with, the Bible points to ordinary Christian experience and calls it a foretaste of what is to come. 'You ... were sealed with the promised Holy Spirit, which is the guarantee of our inheritance until we acquire possession of it' (Ephesians 1:13f.). In modern Greek, the word translated here 'guarantee' is used for an engagement ring, and in ancient Greek it meant a pledge or a down-payment. Our knowledge of the risen Lord Jesus today is a glimpse – and *only* a glimpse – of the life we will share with him in the resurrection.

Secondly, instead of speculating about the nature of the new man, the New Testament looks to Jesus and says: 'It does not yet appear what we shall be, but we know that when he appears we shall be like him, for we shall see him as he is' (1 John 3:2). We shall not be toy replicas of Christ, but true reflections of his character. 'As was the man of dust (Adam), so are those who are of the dust; and as is the man of heaven (Jesus), so are those who are of heaven. Just as we have borne the image of the man of dust, we shall also bear the image of the man of heaven' (1 Corinthians 15:48f.).

Now in that chapter of 1 Corinthians, Paul sees in the

resurrection of Jesus a further clue to our resurrection life. 'Christ', he says, 'has been raised from the dead, the first fruits of those who have fallen asleep' (verse 20). Then he goes on, 'But some one will ask, "How are the dead raised? With what kind of body do they come?" You foolish man!' (No offence meant; personally I think it is a perfectly natural question, but I suppose the answer is fairly obvious when you think about it!) 'What you sow does not come to life unless it dies. And what you sow is not the body which is to be, but a bare kernel, perhaps of wheat or of some other grain ... So it is with the resurrection of the dead. What is sown is perishable, what is raised is imperishable. It is sown in dishonour, it is raised in glory. It is sown in weakness, it is raised in power. It is sown a physical body, it is raised a spiritual body' (verses 35ff., 42ff.).

Jesus' resurrection body was different from his physical body, but continuous with it. He was recognizable in his familiar actions and words, yet he seemed unlimited by time and space. In a preview of the resurrection, Peter, James and John saw Jesus transfigured, shining with the glory and splendour of the transcendent presence of God (Mark 9:1-8).

And whatever else heaven actually is, it is the manifest presence of God which Christians will one day share. There we will be free from the hunger and thirst, the pain and the tears, the frustration of weakness and the sins of wilfulness which dog our steps in the present life (Revelation 7:16; 21:4). There we shall find our true identity; 'To him who conquers ... I will give him a white stone, with a new name written on the stone which no one knows except him who receives it' (Revelation 2:17). The *imago Dei*, the image of God, will be restored within a newly created environment. It is more than a coincidence, perhaps, that a fully developed, metamorphosed insect is called an *imago*. As the crawling earthbound caterpillar is metamorphosed into a soaring butterfly, so we shall become, not flying angels with harps, but the fully fledged humans, full of character and understanding but without sin, that God created us to be.

But we shall find no encouragement in the Bible to dwell exclusively on our future prospects and neglect the present; there is no command to await the coming of Jesus and the resurrection in the seclusion of a mountain hideaway. The glimpses of the future which we are given are incentives to life in the present. We know where we are going: life cannot be pointless and hopeless even though it may be tough. We have a glorious future awaiting us; we dare not be inglorious now.

For the grace of God has appeared for the salvation of all men, training us to renounce irreligion and worldly passions, and to live sober, upright, and godly lives in this world, awaiting our blessed hope, the appearing of the glory of our great God and Saviour Jesus Christ, who gave himself for us to redeem us from all iniquity and to purify for himself a people of his own who are zealous for good deeds (Titus 2:11 ff.).

Follow-up

1. Ephesians 2 is probably the fullest yet briefest summary of the Christian gospel in the whole Bible. Read it through carefully; what does Paul tell us about (a) the state of the non-Christian; (b) the nature of salvation; (c) the purpose of salvation?

2. What should be our attitude to our sins and failings after we become Christians? Romans 6:1–4; 15:1f.; Ephesians 4:22–32; 1 John 1:5–2:6.

3. What else can you discover from the New Testament about the nature of heaven? John 14:1–7; 1 Corinthians 15:51–58; Philippians 1:21–24; 1 Thessalonians 4:13–18; Revelation 7:9–17; 21:1–8; 22:1–5.

References

[1] Charles Reich, *The greening of America* (Allen Lane, The Penguin Press, 1971), chapters 9 and 10.

[2] Gordon Rattray-Taylor, *Rethink* (Secker and Warburg, 1972), p. 153.

[3] C. S. Lewis, *Undeceptions* (Bles, 1971), p. 35.

[4] W. F. Batt (ed.), *Facing the facts* (IVP, 1964), p. 30.

[5] Friedrich Nietzsche, *Thus spake Zarathustra* (George Allen and Unwin, 1932), p. 67.

Postscript for bookworms

Here is a small selection of books on the biblical understanding
of man which I personally have found helpful and which I
believe you will too. It is by no means an exhaustive list, and I
have compiled it with the inquisitive general reader in mind,
and not the expert theologian. Some of the titles are out of
print but can often be picked up secondhand. The dates refer
to the editions I have consulted.

General books

Charles Martin's paperback *How human can you get?* (IVP,
1973) introduces the Christian-humanist debate, as does *What
is human?* by T. M. Kitwood (IVP, 1970) at a deeper level. A
heavyweight publication is G. C. Berkouwer's *Man: the
image of God* (IVP, 1972), but this is a detailed study of theological interpretations of man. A classic worth its dusty weight
in gold is John Laidlaw, *The Bible doctrine of man* (T. and T.
Clark, 1895). Another oldie, priceless for its concise introduction to the historical debates, is *The Christian estimate of man* by
Sidney Cave (Duckworth, 1944). If you have been a Christian
for a while, try Thomas Boston, *Human nature in its fourfold state*
(Banner of Truth, 1964); it is a reprint of an eighteenth-century
devotional treatise.

As you will have realized, some understanding of the
cultural and philosophical background of various periods of
church history is useful if we are to discern what is helpful

and true in the various pronouncements and assertions that are made. Colin Brown gives a readable survey in his book *Philosophy and the Christian faith* (IVP, 1969), and for insight into current thought, Os Guinness' *The dust of death* (IVP, 1973) is unbeatable, with Francis Schaeffer, *The God who is there* (Hodder and Stoughton, 1970) running a close second.

Books on specific subjects

Chapter 1: the creation: Books abound on the problem of creation; if you want a balanced picture steer clear of all except a few standard ones. Francis Schaeffer in *Genesis in space and time* (Hodder and Stoughton, 1973) asserts the historicity of Genesis and helpfully explains creation and the fall. E. K. V. Pearce is a clergyman-cum-anthropologist whose book *Who was Adam?* (Paternoster Press, 1969) deserves a wider audience; he examines the Bible text in the light of anthropological and archaeological discovery. The philosophical and technical problems which crop up in the science-and-religion debate have been given an airing by Donald MacKay in *The clockwork image* (IVP, 1974).

Chapter 2: the fall: Try your daily newspaper! And for a powerful challenge (not recommended for those who feel sick at the sight of the word 'sin'), read Ralph Venning, *The plague of plagues* (Banner of Truth, 1965); like Boston, it is a Puritan reprint.

Chapter 3: the image of God: Francis Schaeffer's slim volume *Back to freedom and dignity* (Hodder and Stoughton, 1973) asserts the biblical concept of the image of God over current deterministic views.

Chapter 4: male and female: There have been many books on the Christian view of sex and marriage in recent years, but I would put all my money on Otto Piper's *The biblical view of sex and marriage* (Nisbet, 1960). It is a little dated but still valuable.

If your money won't stretch that far, Walter Trobisch's *I married you* (IVP, 1972) is the best thing written at a popular level.

Chapter 5: man in society: The Christian in the world is, at the time of writing, becoming a big talking-point. Several books have been written on life-style and Christian responsibility for society. All the more reason, therefore, to get hold of A. N. Triton's *Whose world?* (IVP, 1970) which will give you a basic grounding in the major biblical principles before you go on to whatever is in vogue.

Chapter 7: mind and heart: I mentioned A. T. Schofield in the text, and his little paperback *Christian sanity*, written at the turn of the century, is full of common sense and helpful exposition. I wish it was twice as long (reissued by Oliphants, 1965). John Stott's *Your mind matters* (IVP, 1972) is only a booklet, but as with anything by this man, he packs a great deal into a short space.

Chapter 9: the new creation: If you are not a Christian, or if you have become one only recently, then try another of John Stott's books, *Basic Christianity* (IVP, 1958). Dick France introduces Jesus to us in *The man they crucified* (IVP, 1975) and Michael Green investigates the resurrection in *Man alive!* (IVP, 1967). Michael Griffiths' little classic *Take my life* (IVP, 1967) would be ideal to pick up as soon as you have put this book down.